(E)Dentity

Fountainhead Press V Series

Edited by
Stephanie Vie

FOUNTAINHEAD
PRESS

Our green initiatives include:

Electronic Products
We deliver products in non-paper form whenever possible. This includes pdf downloadables, flash drives, & CDs.

Electronic Samples
We use Xample, a new electronic sampling system. Instructor samples are sent via a personalized web page that links to pdf downloads.

FSC Certified Printers
All of our printers are certified by the Forest Service Council which promotes environmentally and socially responsible management of the world's forests. This program allows consumer groups, individual consumers, and businesses to work together hand-in-hand to promote responsible use of the world's forests as a renewable and sustainable resource.

Recycled Paper
Most of our products are printed on a minimum of 30% post-consumer waste recycled paper.

Support of Green Causes
When we do print, we donate a portion of our revenue to green causes. Listed below are a few of the organizations that have received donations from Fountainhead Press. We welcome your feedback and suggestions for contributions, as we are always searching for worthy initiatives.
Rainforest 2 Reef
Environmental Working Group

Design by Susan Moore

For information, please call or write:

1-800-586-0330

Fountainhead Press
Southlake, TX 76092

Web Site: www.fountainheadpress.com
E-mail: customerservice@fountainheadpress.com

First Edition

ISBN: 978-1-59871-457-9

Printed in the United States of America

INTRODUCTION TO THE FOUNTAINHEAD PRESS V SERIES

BY BROOKE ROLLINS AND LEE BAUKNIGHT
Series Editors

The *Fountainhead Press V Series* is a new collection of single-topic readers that takes a unique look at some of today's most pressing issues. Designed to give writing students a more nuanced introduction to public discourse—on the environment, on food, and on digital life, to name a few of the topics—the books feature writing, research, and invention prompts that can be adapted to nearly any kind of college writing class. Each *V Series* textbook focuses on a single issue and includes multi-genre and multimodal readings and assignments that move the discourse beyond the most familiar patterns of debate—patterns usually fettered by entrenched positions and often obsessed with "winning."

The ultimate goal of the series is to help writing students—who tend to hover on the periphery of public discourse—think, explore, find their voices, and skillfully compose texts in a variety of media and genres. Not only do the books help students think about compelling issues and how they might address them, they also give students the practice they need to develop their research, rhetorical, and writing skills. Together, the readings, prompts, and longer assignments show students how to add their voices to the conversations about these issues in meaningful and productive ways.

With enough readings and composing tasks to sustain an entire quarter or semester, and inexpensive enough to be used in combination with other rhetorics and readers, the *Fountainhead Press V Series* provides instructors with the flexibility to build the writing courses they want and need to teach. An instructor interested in deeply exploring environmental issues, for example, could design a semester- or quarter-long course using *Green*, the first of the *V Series* texts. On the other hand, an instructor who wanted to teach discrete units on different issues could use two or more of the *V Series* books. In either case, the texts would give students ample opportunity—and a variety of ways—to engage with the issues at hand.

The *V Series* uses the term "composition" in its broadest sense. Of course, the textbooks provide students plenty of opportunities to write, but they also include assignments that take students beyond the page. Books in the series encourage students to explore other modes of communication by prompting them to design web sites, for example; to produce videos, posters, and presentations; to conduct primary and secondary research; and to develop projects with community partners that might incorporate any number of these skills. Ultimately, we have designed the *Fountainhead Press V Series* to work for teachers and students. With their carefully chosen readings, built-in flexibility, and sound rhetorical grounding, the *V Series* books would be a dynamic and user-friendly addition to any writing class.

TABLE OF CONTENTS

INTRODUCTION
YOUR (E)DENTITY

By Stephanie Vie

Who are you? What are you like? How do you define yourself? How might others label you? These questions and more assist us in forming our personal identities; these identities differentiate us from others and help carve out our own niches. But today, as we live more and more of our lives in online spaces, we also carry with us an "(e)dentity", an electronic identity composed of the digital traces left behind as we participate in virtual worlds. Every time you upload a picture to a social networking site, create an avatar in an online game, blog or tweet about your life, or buy something online, you generate digital traces that, when examined, form your (e)dentity.

Many of these digital traces are created unconsciously; when you reply to an e-mail or request a movie from Netflix, you probably do not consider that part of your (e)dentity, yet those actions leave digital footprints that can be mined for data by various companies and corporate entities. For example, if you have a Gmail account, next time you open an e-mail, take a look at the advertisements on the right-hand side of the screen; they will change based on keywords in the e-mail you are reading. The ads are derived from portions of your (e)dentity and targeted to what the system believes you might be interested in. As a result, our digital traces can leave us vulnerable to data mining, identity theft, and privacy loss. Yet our (e)dentities also help us search for friends and be searched for by others, allowing us to form relationships

and reconnect with people from our pasts. Even after our deaths, our online identities may still be visible in our social networking profiles that remain online.

It is easy to see that living a life online requires us to balance carefully our need for privacy with our desire to connect with others. The formation of our (e)dentities through the digital traces we leave has become such a natural part of our lives that it is hard to remember a time before social networking, before e-mail, and before instant messaging. Just think about the fact that Facebook has only been around since 2004 (and only open to the general public since 2006), yet it has become firmly entrenched in millions of peoples' lives—over five hundred million as of July 2010 according to Facebook founder Mark Zuckerberg. The ease with which we can look up and chat with friends, remember birthdays, and maintain a growing list of social connections is something we may take for granted, forgetting that it was not always this way. Also, our collective memory of how privacy and identity has been shaped by online sites like Facebook can sometimes be shaky; when the "News Feed" feature was introduced in September 2006, thousands of users were outraged, concerned that changes in their relationship status, conversations with other users, and so on were now immediately visible to everyone else in their network. Now imagine Facebook without that feature today. Difficult, isn't it? We have grown comfortable with the changes and learned to adjust—yet the underlying issues of privacy and (e)dentity never went away. We have simply adjusted to those, too.

It is not only social networking sites that have fundamentally altered our understandings of identity, (e)dentity, privacy, and relationships; virtual spaces like online gaming sites, blogs, wikis, Twitter, and others have also had major roles in shaping the ways we communicate with and about others both online and off. Since the first blogs in the late nineties, we have seen blogging affect our world at societal and personal levels. Blogs have played a part in the decline of traditional print journalism; some have been banned in totalitarian regimes; some bloggers have been fired, even imprisoned, for what they have written. Social media have also played major parts in world revolutions. In 2009, Twitter users in

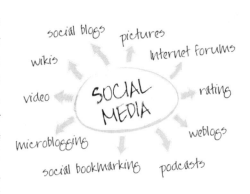

Iran objected to the reelection of President Mahmoud Ahmadinejad; similarly, Egyptian protesters in early 2011 ousted President Hosni Mubarak after his nearly thirty-year reign. Closer to home, an event that clearly illustrated both the power and the limitations of social media was the flood of rapid reactions to the shooting of U. S. Congresswoman Gabrielle Giffords on January 8, 2011. While the dissemination of information was nearly instantaneous, Twitter coverage of this event shows how the usual filters that ensure the veracity of news reports are not always in use in online spaces. Today, as we navigate the sea of information surrounding us, it is even more important that we stop to consider contextual clues and not rush to conclusions.

Despite the complexities that social media have introduced to our communication styles, social media have offered many benefits as well; they have helped connect individuals with similar interests and offered a more rapid, grassroots-level way to circulate news. It is no wonder that in 2006, *Time* magazine chose as its "Person of the Year" simply "you." The cover featured a reflective panel that mirrored the reader's face. *Time* noted that "2006 gave us some ideas. This is an opportunity to build a new kind of international understanding, not politician to politician, great man to great man, but citizen to citizen, person to person." We can see the results of such a person-to-person form of communication in sites like Wikipedia, the go-to source for many to look up information quickly. Its creation challenged many of our views about the reliability and validity of collaboratively written materials that have not gone through traditional peer review (where information is vetted and evaluated by a group of individuals qualified, based on their scholarly achievements, to assess the work). The wiki software itself has brought into question the differences between single-authored, multiple-authored, and anonymous writing. Much like blogs, social networking sites, and Twitter, wikis continue to play a role in our understandings of what it means to communicate in the twenty-first century.

As you can imagine, there are no easy answers to the questions raised by our lives online; like our personal identities and our (e)dentities, virtual spaces are constantly changing and are both shaping us and being shaped by us. While this is happening, though, we are continuously in conversation with each other, and this book, *(E)dentity*, reflects that ongoing conversation. The readings featured here do not attempt to present definitive answers on questions of privacy, identity, and connectivity that have emerged from our lives online; instead, these readings form a conversation that invites you to join in and consider how your voice might connect to those already speaking. Rather than focusing on scholarly narratives, *(E)dentity* draws from multiple sources: newspapers, magazines, blog posts, online comics, and even Twitter feeds. Some are humorous, some serious, some playful, and some thought-provoking; all are meant to illustrate the multiplicity of voices participating in the ongoing conversation about online life and identity.

Along the way you will find research, invention, and composing prompts to help you join the conversation. Much like the readings provided in this book, the kinds of composing you will be prompted to do will move in many ways beyond what you might think of as traditional academic writing. You might be asked to write a blog post, analyze a series of Twitter "tweets," create an avatar, examine a webcomic, or reflect on playing video games. Communication in a digital age has adapted in many ways to the new forms of media we encounter daily and the prompts throughout *(E)dentity* reflect a more contemporary understanding of what writing might look like today.

One way to get started in this book and consider how writing has changed today is to explore how we sort information and content on the web through visualization tools such as tag clouds. (A tag cloud is a visual depiction of the words used in a piece of writing; the greater the frequency with which a word is used, the larger it appears in the cloud.) The first exercise below asks you to choose your own writing or a written piece found online and explore a new way to focus on writing. Similarly, the second exercise below asks you to begin your journey through this book by reflecting on your own (e)dentity. As you continue through *(E)dentity* and read further, you will add additional layers of understanding and meaning to your initial conception of your (e)dentity, just as each time you participate in online spaces you add more layers to your online identity.

Choose a brief piece of writing that you have composed or, alternatively, find one online. Visit http://www.wordle.net and paste in the text that you have chosen, then analyze the visual results—the "tag cloud" created from your text. The most common words will appear in a larger font size to indicate that they occur more often. What are your most common words? Your least common words will appear in a smaller font. What are they? Does the word frequency seem to match up with the overall theme or argument of the piece? How does your understanding of the text change when you visualize it differently like this? How could you use tag clouds to think through different steps of the writing process—from brainstorming to prewriting to revision?

Begin by listing ten words that define you. Weave those words into a short response that describes who you are, what you believe in, what you stand for, what you are like, and so on. Next, make a second list of ten words that describe your online presence—your (e)dentity. Keep in mind that your (e)dentity is formed through the traces left behind from your online activities and interactions. Thus you might list words that relate to your communication activities through e-mail, Twitter, blogging, and social networking; you might also list words that reflect how you've crafted a digital persona that can be seen in your social networking profiles, pictures of you online, and so on. Compose a second short response that weaves in the words from your second list about your (e)dentity.

Now, examine your two responses and reflect on the following questions in a brief essay: Is there significant overlap between how you have described yourself in your two responses? What words appear twice? What words are new? Write a brief reflection exploring to what extent your online identity seems to differ from your offline identity and why.

(E)DENTITY

John Palfrey is a Professor of Law and Vice Dean for Library and Information Resources at Harvard Law School; Urs Gasser is the Berkman Center for Internet & Society's Executive Director at Harvard University. Together they are co-authors of the book Born Digital: Understanding the First Generation of Digital Natives, *published in 2008, which attempts to deepen our understandings of the term "digital native" by complicating it and combating generalizations about technology and today's youth.*

excerpt from

BORN DIGITAL: UNDERSTANDING THE FIRST GENERATION OF DIGITAL NATIVES

By John Palfrey and Urs Gasser

You see them everywhere. The teenage girl with the iPod, sitting across from you on the subway, frenetically typing messages into her cell phone. The whiz kid summer intern in your office who knows what to do when your e-mail client crashes. The eight-year-old who can beat you at any video game on the market—and types faster than you do, too. Even your niece's newborn baby in London, whom you've never met, but with whom you have bonded nonetheless, owing to the new batch of baby photos that arrive each week.

All of them are "Digital Natives." They were all born after 1980, when social digital technologies, such as Usenet and bulletin board systems, came online. They all have access to networked digital technologies. And they all have the skills to use those technologies. (Except for the baby—but she'll learn soon enough.)

Chances are, you've been impressed with some of the skills these Digital Natives possess. Maybe your young assistant has shown you a hilarious political satire online that you never would have found on your own, or made presentation materials for you that make your own PowerPoint slides seem medieval by comparison. Maybe your son has Photoshopped a cloud out of a family vacation photo and turned it into the perfect Christmas card. Maybe that eight-year-old made a funny video on her own that tens of thousands of people watched on YouTube.

But there's also a good chance that a Digital Native has annoyed you. That same assistant, perhaps, writes inappropriately casual e-mails to your clients—and somehow still doesn't know how to put together an actual *printed* letter. Or maybe your daughter never comes down for dinner on time because she's always busy online, chatting with her friends. And when she does come down to dinner, she won't stop texting those same friends under the table.

Maybe you're even a bit frightened by these Digital Natives. Your son has told you, perhaps, that a boy in his ninth-grade class is putting up scary, violent messages on his Web page. Or you heard about that ring of college kids who hacked into a company website and stole 487 credit-card numbers before getting caught by police.

There is one thing you know for sure: These kids are different. They study, work, write, and interact with each other in ways that are very different from the ways that you did growing up. They read blogs rather than newspapers. They often meet each other online before they meet in person. They probably don't even know what a library card looks like, much less have one; and if they do, they've probably never used it. They get their music online—often for free, illegally—rather than buying it in record stores. They're more likely to send an instant message (IM) than to pick up the telephone to arrange a date later in the afternoon. They adopt and pal around with virtual Neopets online instead of pound puppies. And they're connected to one another by a common culture. Major aspects of their lives—social interactions, friendships, civic activities—are mediated by digital technologies. And they've never known any other way of life.

Beginning in the late 1970s, the world began to change—and fast. The first online bulletin board system (or "BBS," for short) let people with clunky computer equipment and access to telephone lines swap documents, read news online, and send one another messages. Usenet groups, organized around topics of interest to communities of users, became popular in the early 1980s. E-mail began to enter popular usage later in the 1980s. The World Wide Web made its debut in 1991, with easy-to-use browsers widely accessible a few years after. Search engines, portals and e-commerce sites hit the scene in the last 1990s. By the turn of the millennium, the first social networks and blogs cropped up online. In 2001, Polaroid declared bankruptcy, just as sales of digital cameras started to take off. In 2006, Tower Records liquidated its stores; by 2008, iTunes had become the largest music retailer in the United States. Today, most young people in many societies around the world carry mobile devices—cell phone, Sidekicks, iPhones—at all times, and these devices don't just make phone calls; they also send text messages, surf the Internet, and download music.

This is the most rapid period of technological transformation ever, at least when it comes to information. The Chinese invented the printing press several *centuries* before Johannes Gutenberg developed the European printing press in the mid-1400s and churned out his first Bibles. Few people could afford the printed books made possible by presses for another several centuries. By contrast, the invention and adoption of digital technologies by more than a billion people worldwide has occurred over the span of a few decades. Despite the saturation of digital technologies in many cultures, no generation has yet lived from cradle to grave in the digital era.

No major aspect of modern life is untouched by the way many of us now use information technologies. Business, for instance, can be done more quickly and over greater distances, often with much less capital required to get up and running. Politicians e-mail their constituents, offer video introductions to their campaigns on their websites, and provide volunteers with sophisticated digital tools to organize events on their own. Even religion is being transformed: Priests and pastors, imams, rabbis, gurus, and even Buddhist monks have begun to reach their faithful through their weblogs.

Most notable, however, is the way the digital era has transformed how people live their lives and relate to one another and to the work around them. Some older people were there at the start, and these "Digital Settlers"—though not native to the digital environment, because they grew up in an analog-only world—have helped to shape its contours. These older people are online, too, and often quite sophisticated in their use of these technologies, but they also continue to rely heavily on traditional, analog forms of interaction. Others less familiar with this environment, "Digital Immigrants," learned how to e-mail and use social networks late in life. You know them by the lame jokes and warnings about urban myths that they still forward to large cc: lists. Those who were born digital don't remember a world in which letters were printed and sent, much less handwritten, or where people met up at formal dances rather than on Facebook. The changing nature of human relationships is second nature to some, and learned behaviors to others.

This narrative is about those who wear the earbuds of an iPod on the subway to their first job, not those of us who still remember how to operate a Sony Walkman or remember buying LPs or eight-track tapes. Much is changing beyond just how much young people pay (or don't pay) for their music. The young people becoming university students and new entrants in the workforce, while living much of their lives online, are different from us along many dimensions. Unlike those of us just a shade older, this new generation didn't have to relearn anything to live lives of digital immersion. They learned in digital the first time around; they only know a world that is digital.

Unlike most Digital Immigrants, Digital Natives live much of their lives online, without distinguishing between the online and the offline. Instead of thinking of their digital identity and their real-space identity as separate things, they just have an identity (with representations in two, or three, or more different spaces). They are joined by a set of common practices, including the amount of time they spend using digital technologies, their tendency to multitask, their tendency to express themselves and relate to one another in ways mediated by digital technologies, and their pattern of using the technologies to access and use information and create new knowledge and art forms. For these young people, new digital technologies—computers, cell phones, Sidekicks—are primary mediators of human-to-human connections. They have created a 24/7 network that blends the human with the technical to a degree we haven't experienced before, and it is transforming human relationships in fundamental ways. They feel as comfortable in online spaces as they do in offline ones. They don't think of their hybrid lives as anything remarkable. Digital Natives haven't known anything but a life connected to one another, and to the world of bits, in this manner.

Digital Natives are constantly connected. They have plenty of friends, in real space and in the virtual worlds—indeed, a growing collection of friends they keep a count of, often for the rest of the world to see, in their online social network sites.[1] Even as they sleep, connections are made online, in the background; they wake up to find them each day. Sometimes, these connections are to people the Digital Native would never have had a chance to meet in the offline world. Through social network sites, Digital Natives connect with and IM and share photos with friends all over the world. They may also collaborate creatively or politically in ways that would have been impossible thirty years ago. But in the course of this relentless connectivity, the very nature of relationships—even what it means to "befriend" someone—is changing. Online friendships are based on many of the same things as traditional friendships—shared interests, frequent interaction—but they nonetheless have a very different tenor: They are often fleeting; they are easy to enter into and easy to leave, without so much as a goodbye; and they are also perhaps enduring in ways we have yet to understand.

Digital natives don't just experience friendship differently from their parents; they also relate to information differently. Consider the way Digital Natives experience music. Not so long ago, teenagers would go to a friend's house to listen to a new record. Or music could signal a shared intimacy: A teenage girl would give her new boyfriend a mixed tape, with song names carefully written onto the cassette lining, to signal her growing affection. Not everything has changed: Digital Natives still listen to copious amounts of music. And they still share lots of music. But the experience is far less likely than before to take place in physical space, with friends hanging out together to listen to a stereo system. The network lets them share music that they each, then, can hear through headphones, walking down the street or in their dorm rooms, mediated by an iPod or the iTunes Music System on their hard drive. The mixed tape has given way to the playlist, shared with friends and strangers alike through social networks online. A generation has come to expect music to be digitally formatted, often free for the taking, and endlessly shareable and portable.

Digital Natives are tremendously creative. It is impossible to say whether they are more or less creative than prior generations, but one thing is certain: They express themselves creatively in ways that are very different from the ways their parents did at their age. Many Digital Natives perceive information to be malleable; it is something they can control and reshape in new and interesting ways. That might mean editing a profile on MySpace or encyclopedia entries on Wikipedia, making a movie or online video, or downloading a hot music track—whether lawfully not. Whether or not they realize it, they have come to have a degree of control over their cultural environment that is unprecedented. Digital Natives can learn how to use a new software program in a snap. They seemingly can take, upload, and edit pictures to share with friends online in their sleep. Digital Natives, at their most creative, are creating parallel worlds on sites like Second Life. And after they do, they record parts of that world and post a video of it on YouTube (if they live in California) or Daily Motion (if they live in Cannes) in a new art form called "machinima." Digital Natives can rework media, using off-the-shelf computer programs, in ways that would have seemed impossible a few short decades ago.

Digital Natives are coming to rely upon this connected space for virtually all of the information they need to live their lives. Research once meant a trip to a library to paw through a musty card catalog and puzzle over the Dewey Decimal System to find a book to pull off the shelves. Now, research means a Google search—and, for most, a visit to Wikipedia before diving deeper into a topic. They simply open a browser, punch in a search term, and dive away until they find what they want—or what they thought they wanted. Most Digital Natives don't buy the newspaper—ever. It's not that they don't read the news, it's just that they get it in new ways and in a wide variety of formats. And they have little use for those big maps you have to fold on the creases, or for TV listings, travel guides, or pamphlets of any sort; the print versions are not obsolete, but they do strike Digital Natives as rather quaint. These changes, to be sure, are not all good, but they will be enduring.

Indeed, many aspects of the way in which Digital Natives lead their lives are cause for concern. Digital Natives' ideas about privacy, for instance, are different from those of their parents and grandparents. In the process of spending so much time in this digitally connected environment, Digital Natives are leaving more traces of themselves in public places online. At their best, they show off who they aspire to be and put their most creative selves before the world. At their worst, they put information online that may put them in danger, or that could humiliate them in years to come. With every hour they log online, they are leaving more tracks for marketers—and pedophiles, for that matter—to follow. There's more about them for admissions officers and potential employers—and potential dates—to find. The repercussions of these changes, in the decades to come, will be profound for all of us. But those who are growing up as Digital Natives are on track to pay the highest price.

Digital Natives will move markets and transform industries, education and global politics. The changes they bring about as they move into the workforce could have an immensely positive effect on the world we live in. By and large, the digital revolution has already made this world a better place. And Digital Natives have every chance of propelling society further forward in myriad ways—if we let them.

But make no mistake: We are at a crossroads. There are two possible paths before us—one in which we destroy what is great about the Internet and about how young people use it, and one in which we make smart choices and head toward a bright future in a digital age. The stakes of our actions today are very high. The choices that we are making now will govern how our children and grandchildren live their lives in many important ways: how they shape their identities, protect their privacy, and keep themselves safe; how they create, understand, and shape the information that underlies the decision-making of their generation; and how they learn, innovate, and take responsibility as citizens. On one of these paths, we seem to constrain their creativity, self-expression, and innovation in public and private spheres; on the other, we embrace these things while minimizing the dangers that come with the new era.

Fear is the single biggest obstacle to getting started on that second path, the one where we realize the potential of digital technology and the way that Digital Natives are using it. Parents, educators, and psychologists all have legitimate reasons to worry about the digital environment in which young people are spending so much of their time. So do corporations, who see their revenues at risk in industry after industry—recorded entertainment, telephony, newspapers, and on and on. Lawmakers, responding to this sense of crisis, fear that they will pay a high price if they fail to act in the traditional manner to right these wrongs.

The media feeds this fear. News coverage is saturated with frightening stories of cyberbullying, online predators, Internet addiction, and online pornography. Of course parents worry. Parents worry most that their digitally connected kids are at risk of abduction when they spend hours a day in an uncontrolled digital environment where few things are precisely as they seem at first glance. They worry, too, about bullying that their children may encounter online, addiction to violent video games, and access to pornographic and hateful images.

Parents aren't the only ones who fear the impact of the Internet on young people. Teachers worry that they are out of step with the Digital Natives they are teaching, that the skills they have imparted over time are becoming either lost or obsolete, and that the pedagogy of our educational system cannot keep up with the changes in the digital landscape. Librarians, too, are reimagining their role: Instead of primarily organizing book titles in musty card catalogs and shelving the books in the stacks, they serve as guides to an increasingly variegated information environment. Companies in the entertainment industry worry that they'll lose their profits to piracy, and newspaper execs fear their readers are turning to Drudge, Google, blogs, or worse for their news.

As parents of Digital Natives, we take both the challenges and the opportunities of digital culture seriously. We share the concerns of many parents about the threats to the privacy of our children, to their safety, and to their education. We worry about the crush of too much information and the impact of violent games and images online. But as a culture of fear emerges around the online environment, we must put these real threats into perspective; our children and future generations have tremendous opportunities in store for them, not in spite of the digital age, but because of it.

We see promise in the way that Digital Natives are interacting with digital information, expressing themselves in social environments, creating new art forms, dreaming up new business models, and starting new activist ventures. The purpose of this book is to separate what we need to worry about from what's not so scary, what we ought to resist from what we ought to embrace.

There is a huge risk that we, as a society, will fail to harness the good that can come from these opportunities as we seek to head off the worst of the problems. Fear, in many cases, is leading to overreaction, which in turn could give rise to greater problems as young people take detours around the roadblocks we think we are erecting. Instead of emphasizing education and giving young people the tools and skills they need to keep themselves safe, our lawmakers talk about banning certain websites or keeping kids under eighteen out of social networks. Instead of trying to figure out what's going on with kids and digital media, the entertainment industry has gone to war against them, suing its young customers by the tens of thousands. Instead of preparing kids to manage a complex and exploding information environment, governments around the world are passing laws against certain kinds of publications, making the banning of books look like a quaint, harmless activity. At the same time, we do next to nothing in terms of taking the kinds of steps that need to be taken if we are to address the real concerns facing kids.

Our goal in this book is to present the good and the bad in context and to suggest things that all of us—parents, teachers, leaders of companies, and lawmakers—can do to manage this extraordinary transition to a globally connected society without shutting the whole thing down.

The hard problem at the core of this book is how to balance caution with encouragement: How do we take effective steps to protect our children, as well as the interests of others, while allowing those same kids enough room to figure things out on their own? If we can find this balance, in the process we will allow thousands of flowers to bloom online and empower our children to handle problems that will no doubt arise in their future. The solutions that will work are complicated ones. They will involve lots of different groups, including parents and educators as well as technology firms and lawmakers—and, critically, Digital Natives themselves.

In shaping solutions to the problems that arise, we need not think in radically new paradigms. Often, the old-fashioned solutions that have solved similar problems in the past will work in the digital age, too. Those solutions are engaged parenting, a good education, and common sense. A lot of the things we're worried about—bullying, stalking, copyright violations, and so forth—are things we've handled for decades, if not centuries. We can, as a society, handle them in the digital age, too, without the hysteria that has surrounded them. We too often overestimate the ways in which the online environment is different from real space, to our detriment.

Parents and teachers are on the front lines. They have the biggest responsibility and the most important role to play. But too often, parents and teachers aren't even involved in the decisions that young people are making. They cut themselves off from their Digital Native children because the language and cultural barriers are too great. What we hope parents and teachers will begin to understand as they read this book is that the transitional values and common sense that have served them well in the past will be relevant in this new world, too. Rather than banning the technologies or leaving kids to use them on their own in their bedrooms—two of the most common approaches—parents and teachers need to let Digital Natives be their guides into this new, connected way of living. Then the conversation can begin. To many of the questions that arise, common sense is a surprisingly good answer. For the others, we'll need to work together on creative solutions.

That said, parents and teachers need not, and should not, go it alone. As mentioned earlier, Digital Natives, their peers, technology companies, and lawmakers each have a role to play in solving these problems. Imagine a series of concentric circles, with the Digital Native at the center (see Figure 1). In many cases, the Digital Natives themselves are the ones who are best positioned to solve the problems that arise from their digital lives. Of course, it's not always realistic to put Digital Natives in charge, but it's important to start there all the same. One circle out, the family and close friends of a Digital Native can have an impact, whether through guidance (in the case of Internet safety, for instance) or through collaborative development of social norms (in the case of intellectual property). The third circle includes teachers and mentors, who often can have a big impact on how Digital Natives navigate these environments. Fourth, we look to the technology companies that build software and offer services, which can also make a big difference in how these issues play out—and which must act accountably if that difference is going to be for the good. Fifth, we turn to the law and to law enforcement, often powerful instruments but usually blunt ones—and properly seen as a last resort.

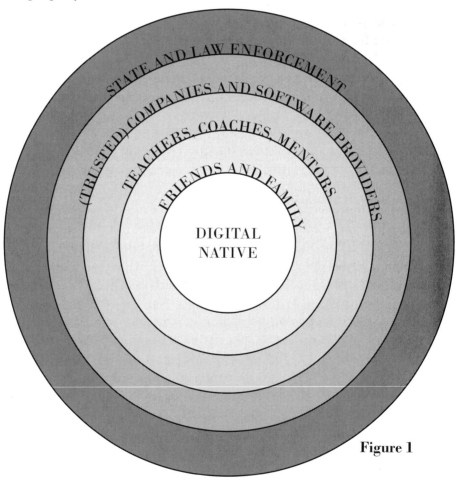

Figure 1

We are not indifferent to the outcome of the many legal, political, and moral debates that this material engages. For one thing, we are both parents of Digital Natives. We care deeply about the world in which they are growing up, about the friendships they will make, about their safety, and how they learn and engage with society at large. We are eager for them to become active, caring, global citizens.

For another thing, we are lawyers. We love the law. We believe strongly that the law is an essential part of organizing our democratic societies in a constructive way. The law is a crucial means to solving many social problems. But we are also lawyers who believe that the limits of law are sharply apparent in the context of many of the problems we are studying there. Despite the uncertainty inherent in predicting the future, now is the time to look ahead, whether as parents, as teachers, or as policymakers, technologists, or Digital Natives, and to shape—without doing harm—the regulatory framework for the emerging digital space in ways that advance the public interest. In some cases, like the surge in online creativity, these trends point to opportunities we should harness. In others, such as the privacy problem or the cyberbullying problem, substantial dangers lurk in the digital future that we ought to head off at the pass. The law is rarely the right answer, but we should not hesitate to use it when it could do more good than harm. Technology companies can be encouraged to do the right thing on their own, especially when they know that future regulation is a possibility if they do not. And it's always important to have law enforcement as a backstop for the worst cases.

In writing this book, we've been trying to capture a picture of something that is already kaleidoscopic in its complexity, and that changes substantially every few months. By the time this book is printed, it will already be starting to go out of date. It will still provide an introduction to the most serious issues of the digital explosion and how they affect our children, as well as a context in which to think about solutions, and these matters will be pertinent for a long time to come. But we did not want to stop there. Therefore, much of our work is online, so that we can update it over time. It's in the form of a wiki—at http://www. digitalnative.org/—and uses the same technology that powers Wikipedia, the extraordinary online encyclopedia and one of the subjects of this book. It is a technology that allows anyone who wants to participate in updating our work to do so.

Our methodology involved a combination of approaches. We learned a great deal from the best research done by others in the field: social scientists, psychologists, neuroscientists, developmental pediatricians, and librarians. We also conducted original research of our own. In order to understand more clearly the issues facing Digital Natives, we conducted a series of focus groups and interviews of young people. Our goal was not to undertake a comprehensive study, but rather to take an in-depth look at the way young people relate to information and one another.

We spoke in detail to young people from around the world about the technologies they use, how they express their identities online, and what they think about privacy and safety. We asked them what they create in digital formats, what they know about intellectual property, how they research new topics and keep tabs on news about the world, and how they interact with one another. In all, we held about 100 conversations with young people in these formal settings. You will hear their voices, through without their names attached, throughout this book. Our research is also grounded in conversations that we held with about 150 additional informants, including other young people, their teachers, librarians, psychologists, and those who study them.

This culture is global in scope and nature. Whether physically based in Rio de Janeiro, Shanghai, Boston, Oslo, or Cape Town, Digital Natives—often young elites—form part of a global culture of their peers. They are connected to each other in terms of how they relate to information, how they relate to new technologies, and how they relate to one another. When they chat with each other, broadcast their latest videos, post messages on their blogs and social network profiles, or share the latest tune over P2P networks, they do so across states, national boundaries, and continents. Parallel to their digital universe, Digital Natives are embedded in regional and local customs, habits, and values. These factors among others—together with the social and economic context and the local laws—are likely to shape the ways in which Digital Natives use digital technology, how they can realize its opportunities, and how they will address the challenges it poses.

While researching and writing this book, we sought to identify both the common threads of the emerging global culture and to take into account regional and local differences. We have each logged hundreds of thousands of miles over the past few years, visiting dozens of countries and hundreds of places to speak with Digital Natives, their parents and teachers, representatives of software companies, and in several cases government officials. We interviewed them about the topics we're addressing in this book. We learned a lot from these conversations, and we hope that the insights that we brought back—from

Eastern Europe, the Middle East, Asia, and Africa, among other destinations—are faithfully reflected in this book in one way or another.

As expensively educated academics in highly connected, wealthy societies, we come from places of great privilege. Both the opportunities and the problems outlined in this book take on different contours from perspectives other than our own. And there are many such other perspectives. Rather than calling Digital Natives a *generation*—an overstatement, especially in light of the fact that only 1 billion of the 6 billion people in the world even have access to digital technologies—we prefer to think of them as a *population*.

One of the most worrying things of all about digital culture is the huge divide it's opening up between the haves and the have nots. This divide is regional: Wealthy countries like the United States and Switzerland have high levels of broadband access, high rates of literacy, and educational systems that (often) emphasize critical thinking. As a result, many kids in wealthy countries are Digital Natives. In the developing world, the technology is less prevalent, electricity often scarce, and literacy rates low, and the number of teachers who know how to instruct kids in the use of technologies in short supply. There's a divide even within rich countries. In the United States, most kids can access the technology itself, but there are huge divides between those children who have the skills to use it effectively and those who do not.

The vast majority of young people born in the world today are not growing up as Digital Natives. There is a yawning participation gap between those who are Digital Natives and those who are the same age, but who are not learning about digital technologies and living their lives in the same way.[2] For billions of people around the world, the problems facing Digital Natives are mere abstractions.

The biggest concern that we highlight in this book is the impact of the participation gap. The digital world offers new opportunities to those who know how to avail themselves of them. These opportunities make possible new forms of creativity, learning, entrepreneurship, and innovation. In the past, many have worried about the "digital divide," the separation between those with access to the network and those without access. This is a persistent problem, but it's not the whole problem. The harder issue arises when you realize that access to the technologies is not enough. Young people need to learn digital literacy—the skills to navigate this complicated, hybrid world that their peers are growing up in. This type of inequality must be overcome. The costs of leaving the participation gap unaddressed over time will be higher than we should be willing to bear.

This story is breaking all around us, around the world, at unprecedented speed. The bad news is that there are no easy answers to the puzzles that Digital Natives encounter as they navigate their digitally mediated lives or to the problem of the participation gap. The good news is that there is a lot that we can do as our children grow up, with them and for them. We each have a role to play in solving these problems. Most important of all, we need to prepare our Digital Natives and other young people to lead the way themselves toward a bright future in the digital age.

REFERENCES

1 See, for example, D.A. Huffaker and S.L. Calvert, "Gender, Identity, and Language Use in Teenage Blogs," *Journal of Computer-Mediated Communication* 10, no. 2 (2005), http://jcmc.indiana.edu/vol10/issue2/huffaker.html.

2 For a scholarly overview of many of the key issues that we address in this chapter, see David Buckingham, ed., *Youth, Identity, and Digital Media* (Cambridge: MIT Press, 2008), a series of fine essays on the changing nature of identity for young people in a digital age. See also Nicola Doring, *Sozialpsychologie des Internet*, 2d ed. (Gottingen: Hofgrede, 2003), pp. 325-402. Doring explains how a given media environment impacts the types of identities we develop, how we communicate about these identities, and how we perceive the identities of others. The medium has an influence on both the personal identity and the social identity.

Invent

After reading Palfrey and Gasser's introduction "Born Digital," consider who might be their intended audience: What type of reader do you believe the authors had in mind when they wrote their piece? How do you know? What textual cues help you understand their intended audience? Do you feel that you are part of the intended audience for either text, and how does that affect your reading?

Collaborate

With a group of classmates, discuss Palfrey and Gasser's definition of "digital natives" and complicate that definition: Are there any groups of people who would be left out of the "digital natives" grouping based on the way the authors define them? Does their definition rely on any generalizations or stereotypes to make its point? Does your group feel that Palfrey and Gasser's definition of "digital natives" applies equally well to everyone in your group or everyone in your classroom—even everyone in your school?

(E)DENTITY

Both Brown and Steven Johnson comment on how literacy has shifted since the dawn of the web, with Johnson refuting widespread concerns that young people today do not read. In his 2005 book, Everything Bad is Good for You: How Today's Popular Culture Is Actually Making Us Smarter, Johnson discusses how popular leisure time activities like watching television and playing video games stimulate our brains because of the growing complexity of these activities. Johnson has written for Wired, Discover Magazine, and Slate and is the author of seven books on technology, science, and popular culture.

DAWN OF THE DIGITAL NATIVES

By Steven Johnson

If you believe a scary US report, reading is on the decline. But, says Steven Johnson, it completely fails to consider the amount that we do every day on our computers.

We've been hearing about the decline of reading for so long now that it's amazing a contemporary teenager can even recognise a book, much less read one. The US (where I am) seems to be cycling through yet another "Johnny can't read" mini-panic, sparked by the release of a National Endowment for the Arts study, called To Read Or Not To Read, which chronicles in exhaustive statistical detail the waning of literary culture and its dire consequences for society. Newspapers dutifully editorialised about America's literacy crisis.

It's the sort of "our kids in peril" story—right up there with threats of MySpace predators—that plays well as a three-minute television newsbite or a three-paragraph op-ed piece. But if you actually read the report, what you find are some startling omissions—omissions that ultimately lead to a heavily distorted view of the Google generation and its prospects.

YOU NEED TO READ IT

The NEA makes a convincing case that both kids and adults are reading fewer books. "Non-required" reading—ie, picking up a book for the fun of it—is down 7% since 1992 for all adults, and 12% for 18-24 year olds.

The subtitle of the NEA report—A Question Of National Consequence—would lead you to believe this dramatic drop must have had done significant damage to our reading proficiencies as a society. And indeed, NEA chair Dana Gioia states boldly in his introduction: "The story the data tell is simple, consistent and alarming." But then the data turns out to be complex, inconsistent and not really that alarming at all. As Gioia puts it, in the very next sentence: "Although there has been measurable progress in recent years in reading ability at the elementary school level, all progress appears to halt as children enter their teenage years."

What was that again? There's measurable progress in two of the three age groups reviewed? Actually, it's more than just measurable: if you look at the charts, the single biggest change—either positive or negative—is the spike upwards in reading abilities among nine-year-olds, which jumped seven points from 1999.

But at least there must be an "alarming" drop in reading skills among those 17-year-olds to justify this big report. And there it is: the teenagers are down five points from 1988. But wait, this is all on a scale of 0-500. If you scored it on a standard 100-point exam scale, it's the equivalent of dropping a single point. Not exactly cause for national alarm.

And we're comparing two different generations. Today's teenagers are the nine-year-olds who didn't test all that well back in 1999—presumably because they didn't develop a love of reading that would sustain them through the competing attractions of being a teenager in the digital age. But there's no reason to suspect that the current crop of nine-year-olds won't be much better at sustaining their interest in reading given their current performance.

Comparable non-events appear when you look at prose literacy levels in the adult population: in 1992, 43% of Americans read at an intermediate level; by 2003 the number was slightly higher at 44%. "Proficient" readers dropped slightly, from 15% to 13%. In other words, the distribution is basically unchanged—despite the vast influx of non-native English speakers into the US population during this period.

All of which raises an interesting question: if people are reading less, why haven't scores dropped more dramatically? The answer gets to the most significant sleight of hand of the NEA study: its studies are heavily biased towards words on a printed page.

Odds are that you are reading these words on a computer monitor. Are you not exercising the same cognitive muscles because these words are made out of pixels and not little splotches of ink? According to the NEA you're not, because in almost every study it cites, screen-based reading is excluded from the data. This is a preposterous omission, because of course the single most dramatic change in media habits over the past decade is the huge spike in internet activity.

Yes, we are reading in smaller bites on the screen, often switching back and forth between applications as we do it. A recent study by the British Library of onscreen research activities found that "new forms of 'reading' are emerging as users 'power browse' ... "

And of course we are writing more, and writing in public for strangers: novel readers may have declined by 10%, but the number of bloggers has gone from zero to 25 million. Simply excising screen-based reading from the study altogether is like doing a literacy survey circa 1500 and only counting the amount of time people spent reading scrolls.

All Gioia has to say about the dark matter of electronic reading is this: "Whatever the benefits of newer electronic media, they provide no measurable substitute for the intellectual and personal development initiated and sustained by frequent reading."

TECHNOLOGICAL LITERACY

The only reason the intellectual benefits are not measurable is that they haven't been measured yet. There have been almost no studies that have looked at the potential positive impact of electronic media. Certainly there is every reason to believe that technological literacy correlates strongly with professional success in the information age.

I challenge the NEA to track the economic status of obsessive novel readers and obsessive computer programmers over the next 10 years. Which group will have more professional success in this climate? Which group is more likely to found the next Google or Facebook? Which group is more likely to go from college into a job paying $80,000 (£40,600)?

But the unmeasured skills of the "digital natives" are not just about technological proficiency. One of the few groups that has looked at these issues is the Pew Research Centre, which found in a 2004 study of politics and media use: "Relying on the internet as a source of campaign information is strongly correlated with knowledge about the candidates and the campaign. This is more the case than for other types of media, even accounting for the fact that internet users generally are better educated and more interested politically. And among young people under 30, use of the internet to learn about the campaign has a greater impact on knowledge than does level of education."

In a piece for the *New Yorker*, Caleb Crain manages to write several thousand words about the fate of reading in the modern age with only a few passing references to the computer screen. Unlike the NEA, he at least acknowledges the potential benefits in one brief paragraph: "The internet, happily, does not so far seem to be antagonistic to literacy. Researchers recently gave Michigan children and teenagers home computers in exchange for permission to monitor their internet use. The study found that grades and reading scores rose with the amount of time spent online."

SCREEN SHIFT

The problem with both arguments is that they're fundamentally rehashing the technological opposition of the television age, the kind of opposition that McLuhan wrote about so powerfully back in the 1960s: word versus image, text versus screen. But that long-term decline towards a pure society of image has been reversed by the rise of digital media. What separates the Google generation from postwar generations is the shift from largely image-based passive media to largely text-based interactive media.

We don't know exactly how that will play out in the long run, but thus far, when you look at the demographic patterns of the Google generation, there is not only no cause for alarm: in fact, there's genuine cause for celebration. The twentysomethings in the US—the ones who spent their childhood years engaged with computers and not zoning out in front of the TV—are the least violent, the most politically engaged and the most entrepreneurial since the dawn of the television era.

But if you listen to the NEA, we are perched on the edge of a general meltdown: "The general decline in reading is not merely a cultural issue, though it has enormous consequences for literature and the other arts. It is a serious national problem." A serious national problem with no apparent data to support it. Perhaps the scholars at the NEA should put down their novels and take some statistics classes?

Collaborate

With your classmates, list all of the reading that you have done in the past week. Include both print materials like books, magazines, newspapers, and so on as well as on-screen reading (including blogs, social networking sites, email, Twitter, online news, magazines, and other reading online). Discuss whether the amount of reading you have participated in during the past week is typical of your daily lives or not and why. How do you think you might characterize your reading habits overall?

Compose

Johnson argues that the NEA study on reading habits fails to consider on-screen reading and therefore paints an incorrect picture of the reading habits of students today. Write a letter to the director of the NEA study explaining the kinds of reading that you and your fellow students typically encounter. (You may want to reference the reading list you created with your classmates and describe the amount of reading you and your classmates typically encounter.)

Explore

The NEA's study, "To Read or Not To Read," was released in 2007. Using the Internet and your library resources, research follow-up studies on students' reading habits. Have more recent studies found similar data or have different patterns of reading emerged since 2007?

(E)DENTITY

danah boyd is a Social Media Researcher at Microsoft Research New England and a Fellow at Harvard University's Berkman Center for Internet and Society. She is one of the preeminent researchers on youth, privacy, and social networking, having studied Friendster, LiveJournal, Facebook, MySpace, and many others. Together with frequent co-author Judith Donath, a professor at the MIT Media Lab, boyd examines how one's credibility is affected by listing friendships online through social networks in their 2004 BT Technology Journal article "Public Displays of Affection."

excerpt from

PUBLIC DISPLAYS OF CONNECTION

By Judith Donath and danah boyd

Participants in social network sites create self-descriptive profiles that include their links to other members, creating a visible network of connections—the ostensible purpose of these sites is to use this network to make friends, dates, and business connections. In this paper we explore the social implications of the public display of one's social network. Why do people display their social connections in everyday life, and why do they do so in these networking sites? What do people learn about another's identity through the signal of network display? How does this display facilitate connections, and how does it change the costs and benefits of making and brokering such connections compared to traditional means? The paper includes several design recommendations for future networking sites.

1. INTRODUCTION

'Orkut [1] is an on-line community that connects people through a network of trusted friends'

'Find the people you need through the people you trust'— LinkedIn [2].

'Access people you want to reach through people you know and trust. Spoke Network helps you cultivate a strong personal network by keeping you in touch with your relationships'—Spoke [3].

'Friendster Beta [4]: The new way to meet people. Friendster is an on-line community that connects people through networks of friends for dating or making new friends'.

Social networking sites, in which participants create a self-descriptive profile and make links to other members, have recently become quite popular. 'Networking' is the ostensible purpose of these sites—using one's chain of connections to make new friends, dates, business partners, etc. Underlying all the networking sites are a core set of assumptions—that there is a need for people to make more connections, that using a network of existing connections is the best way to do so, and that making this easy to do is a great benefit.

The first dedicated on-line networking site was sixdegrees.com, which, like today's social networking sites, helped people connect to an extended network of friends of friends and beyond. Sixdegrees.com folded after four years in operation.

Since then, use of the Internet has greatly expanded and today it is much more likely that one's friends and the people one would like to befriend are present in cyberspace. People are accustomed to thinking of the on-line world as a social space. Today, networking sites are suddenly extremely popular.

Social networks—our connections with other people—have many important functions. They are sources of emotional and financial support, and of information about jobs, other people, and the world at large. The types of social networks that develop in different communities have a profound effect on the way people work, the opportunities they have, and the structure of their daily life [5, 6]. There are societies in which network ties reflect a rigid hierarchy and close kinship relationships, and others in which they reflect a mobile culture structured around work and school. Today, we are seeing the advent of social networks formed in cyberspace. People meet in on-line forums and through on-line dating services; they keep in touch with an unprecedentedly large number of people via electronic media.

> people are accustomed to thinking of the on-line world as a social space

In today's society, access to information is a key element of status and power and communication is instant, ubiquitous and mobile. The social networking sites we will be discussing in this paper are a product of this emerging culture. They function both as environments in which these new ties are formed and as depictions of these networks in the display of individual connections.

Social networking sites are on-line environments in which people create a self-descriptive profile and then make links to other people they know on the site, creating a network of personal connections. Participants in social networking sites are usually identified by their real names and often include photographs; their network of connections is displayed as an integral piece of their self-presentation.

The public display of connections is one of the most salient features of the social sites. The focus of this paper is on the social implications of this display. Why do people display their social connections in everyday life—and why do they do so in these networking sites? What do people learn about another's identity through the signal of network display? How does this display facilitate connections, and how does it change the costs and benefits of making and brokering such connections as opposed to doing so via traditional means?

The profile and network of links are the fundamental features of these sites, but the specific instantiation varies from site to site. The examples and observations in this paper are drawn from several contemporary services, including Friendster [4], Orkut [1], Tribe.net [7], Ryze [8] and LinkedIn [2]. These sites undergo frequent redesign and new ones appear often; thus, while we have grounded our analysis on observation [9], we try to speak generally about approaches to design.

Most networking sites share a similar model of interpersonal links—they are mutual, public, unnuanced, and decontextualised:

- links are mutual: if A shows B as a connection, then B has also agreed to show A as a connection,

- the links are public: they are permanently on display for others to see—here, the sites do differ, e.g. LinkedIn allows you to see only the connections made by your immediate links, and only if they allow it, whereas Orkut allows users to explore freely, and others limit network viewings to a still more broad class of friends of friends of friends,

- the links are unnuanced: there is no distinction made between a close relative and a near stranger one chatted with idly on-line one night,

- the links are decontextualised: there is no way of showing only a portion of one's network to some people—some sites do allow users to adjust the closeness by degree of the people who are to be allowed to see their connections, and within that degree everyone can see all connections (there is no ability to segregate one's links), and similarly for one's profile, and a few sites allow limiting parts of the profile to closer connections, but again connection degree is the only distinction made.

The features of the links in the displays of connection—that are public, mutual, unnuanced, and decontextualised—shape the culture that is evolving on these sites.

2. WHAT DOES THE DISPLAY OF CONNECTIONS MEAN?

In the physical world, people display their connections in many ways. They have parties in which they introduce friends who they think would like—or impress—each other [10, 11]. They drop the names of high status acquaintances casually in their conversation. They decorate their refrigerator with photos. Simply appearing in public with one's acquaintances is a display of connection. These displays serve various purposes. The high status name-dropping may be a deliberate ploy to impress the listener of the speaker's importance or ability to effect some action. The refrigerator display may be prompted by the good feeling engendered by memories of pleasant times with friends [12]. The introductions may be done as a favour, as a way of gaining social capital, or as a way of uniting compatible but disconnected circles [10].

> social status, political beliefs, musical taste, etc, may be inferred from the company one keeps

Seeing someone within the context of their connections provides the viewer with information about them. Social status, political beliefs, musical taste, etc, may be inferred from the company one keeps. Furthermore, knowing that someone is connected to people one already knows and trusts is one of the most basic ways of establishing trust with a new relationship [13, 14]. The reliability of the inferences drawn from these displays varies. The social climber who is continuously dropping the names of famous friends may be taking advantage of the listener's inability to verify the stories to create an impressive but imaginary résumé. An intimate dinner party in which the guests are clearly familiar with the host tells much more about the host's social circle than does a giant loft party where the attendees are only vaguely aware of the evening's provenance. The friends depicted in photos on the refrigerator are likely to be just that—but there does exist a market in faux family photos and other material meant to create the impression of aspired to life and history [15]. How important the reliability of the information gleaned from the display of connections is depends on what one is planning to do with it. If one is simply being entertained by a celebrity-laced story, suspension of disbelief is harmless. Yet, if one is being recruited for an investment scheme the desirability of which is based on claims of association with the rich and famous, a deeper analysis would be sensible.

A useful way of analysing the reliability of displays of connections is to think of them in the framework of signaling theory. This theory, developed in both biology [16—18] and economics [19, 20], describes the relationship between a signal and the underlying quality it represents. Most of the qualities we are interested in about other people—Is this person nice? Trustworthy? Can she do this job? Can he be relied on in an emergency? Would she be a good parent? — are not directly observable. Instead, we rely on signals, which are more or less reliably correlated with an underlying quality.

Some signals, often termed honest or assessment signals are inherently reliable because they are costly in terms of the quality they are signalling [18]. For example, a fast and energetic gazelle will exhibit a behaviour called 'stotting' when it sees a predator. Instead of running off, it jumps up and down in place, expending a lot of energy and wasting time. This is a reliable signal of its great speed, for a slower animal could not afford to do this and still outrun the predator. Sometimes, the expense of producing and/or assessing a costly signal is too high, and a less costly but also less reliable signal is used [16]. Such signals are often called conventional signals, because the connection between signal and quality exists by convention rather than necessity. For example, driving an expensive car is a signal of wealth, for to own such a car is quite costly in the domain being signalled, in this case money. Yet a car can be rented and thus a person who is unable to afford to buy a late model Jaguar may still be able to drive one around for a few days. If, however, we add the cost of time for extensive observation, we can increase the reliability of the signal. Seeing someone driving the Jaguar month after month is a more reliable signal of their ownership of it than is a single sighting. If one is only casually interested in the financial status of the driver, a long term investment of time in observing them is unnecessary and undesirable and one is likely to be satisfied with the possibly unreliable information gleaned from the less costly signal of a single observation. If the costs of being mistaken are high, then it is worthwhile to invest in the cost of the assessment signal, which in this case is the monetary investment of the driver and the temporal investment of both driver and observer.

There is another important source of costs in determining the reliability of a signal and that is reputation and the ability of receivers to punish deceivers. In a system where interactions are not repeated and there is no communication within a community, receivers must rely on the signal alone. Yet in a situation in which there is persistent identity and repeated interaction, receivers can punish deceivers through the social mechanism of reputation. Here, the information

> the reliability of social connections can be analyzed in terms of signalling theory

gleaned through experience by an individual can spread through a community. The deceptive signaller then pays a cost in terms of difficulty in finding future interaction partners, etc. This is an important concept in evaluating social networking displays, for they place the individual within a social context that fosters co-operation through the structure of reputation maintenance.

Signalling theory focuses our analysis of the displays of connection in social networking sites on questions such as:

What are the qualities that are being represented by the signal of the network display? What are the costs of producing these displays? What are the benefits that can come from them?

What are the receivers attempting to discern? What are the costs they will bear if the signal is deceptive? It also focuses our attention on the signalling value of the network itself—what are the implications of an articulated social network, that is, a network in which the connections are explicitly depicted, in terms of reputation and the costs that a deceived receiver can impart?

3. DISPLAYING CONNECTIONS TO VERIFY PERSONAL IDENTITY AND ENSURE CO-OPERATION

A public display of connections is an implicit verification of identity. In order to understand the significance of this, we start by briefly discussing how widespread less reliable identity representations are in the on-line world. We then discuss two predictions that can be made about the effect of a public display of connections. First, since one's connections are linked to one's profile, which they have presumably viewed and implicitly verified, it should ensure honest self-presentation. Secondly, since the display makes one's connections and the means of contacting them public, it should ensure co-operative behaviour by putting one's reputation on the line with all transactions, for an unhappy date or client, etc, can easily contact the connections. The section concludes with a discussion of displays of connection and identity theft.

3.1 Verifying personal identity

Identity deception is prevalent in the on-line world. In the real world the body anchors identity, making it both singular and difficult to change. Identity deception, though not unheard of, is difficult—convincingly representing oneself as a member of the opposite gender is quite costly, requiring extensive makeup, costuming, and possibly surgery, while portraying oneself as a different person requires acquiring another's documents, avoiding known acquaintances, and risking a lengthy incarceration. On-line, identity is mutable and unanchored by the body that is its locus in the real world [21]. In many situations, creating pseudonyms has little cost and if one ruins the on-line reputation tied to one screen name, it is simple to acquire a new name and return afresh [22]. Behind the new name is the same problematic person, but the equivalence between the disreputable old name and the clean new name—the fact that they are both names for the same person—is invisible.

In some situations, such as game playing, the ease of creating imaginary personas and unsullied pseudonyms is acceptable. But for many purposes, such as providing support, exchanging goods and services, finding friends and seeking employees, it is not. Here, the cost of being deceived can be quite high, and it is worthwhile for people to assume and demand greater costs in order to be more confident in their belief in the other's identity.

A public display of connections can be viewed as a signal of the reliability of one's identity claims. If I write a description of myself for strangers to read, it is easy to prevaricate. Yet if I take that description and ask a number of people who know me to link to it and implicitly vet it, this should increase the reliability of the description. In theory, the public display of connections found on networking sites should ensure honest self-presentation because one's connections are linked to one's profile; they have both seen it and, implicitly, sanctioned it.

A comparison of identity presentation in contexts with and without social networks can be made by comparing social networking sites and dating sites. Both are used to find dates and both feature self-written profiles. They differ in that the dating sites are pseudonymous and have no display of connection while the network sites feature real names and displays of connection. Dating sites are thriving, with millions of users reportedly every month [23]. Yet there have also been numerous reports of identity deception in such sites, ranging from the relatively innocuous misrepresentation of personal appearance and achievements, to more serious deceptions about marital status and intentions. The costs of creating a deceptive dating site profile are relatively low and are often not in the domain being advertised. For example, stating 'I am a kind, thoughtful and romantic person' does not impose any costs on one's kindness or romantic nature and requires little thought. Social networking sites should be more reliable. The use of one's real name and the network both imply that if one were to prevaricate extensively in one's profile, real acquaintances would see this and presumably, make some rebuke—or at least, one would be embarrassed to be seen exaggerating accomplishments in front of one's friends. More serious deceptions, such as a married person posing as an available single, are far more difficult to perform in a networking site. In order to remain innocent in the eyes of one's friends and family one would need to create a new persona and then surround oneself with invented friends and very weak ties or would need to appear as acutely alone. Appearing on a networking site with a full network of acquaintances is a relatively reliable signal that one's participation on the site is within the boundaries of acceptable behaviour within that network.

Does this mean that the display of connections on social networking sites makes the presentation of identity in these environments very reliable? If the connections listed on the profile were always a) real people who b) knew the subject and c) would impose sanctions on false self-portrayals, then yes, these sites would be quite reliable. Yet these assumptions do not always hold.

- Real people

  It is possible that the connections listed are not real people. There is often little or no verification of people when they sign up to join most networking sites. It is easy to create a false persona; the costs lie in building the network. The determined deceiver can create a series of false profiles and have them link to each other, creating the illusion of a network of well-connected participants. The cost here is the effort required to create these multiple personas. This cost is dependent on the registration requirements of the site and sites that make registration more difficult raise the cost and lower the likelihood of such deception. Today, most sites are free. Some require an invitation from an existing member, but it would be possible simply to invite the made-up profiles oneself. A site that requires an invitation from an existing member AND that keeps the host member's name on the invitee's profile (which is seldom if ever done today) would make the cost of creating a circle of deception higher, by making it possible to trace the chain of links to a real person. While such elaborate deceptions are rare, if the benefits of creating a believable but false persona are high enough, it is likely that they will occur. Sites that value their own reputation as a place where people can find trustworthy others should be cognisant of the value of registration costs and of maintaining invitation chains.

- Who knew the subject

It is possible that the connections are real people, but that they do not know the subject. The culture of the networking sites varies. In some, it is common for strangers to happen upon an interesting profile, and contact the person requesting a connection; in others, it is common for people to link only to others they do know. Linking to externally unknown people became so common on Friendster that the phrase 'she's not my friend, she's my friendster' [9] arose to explain the relationship one has with a person known only through that site. This is not inherently bad—after all, the social sites are designed to help people meet and linking to one another is the obvious action to take upon introduction in this environment. The drawback is that this ease of meeting means that the degree of acquaintanceship signified by a link may be very minimal. If the people on someone's display of connections do not know the subject in real life, they have no way to verify the profile—they, like the receiver, know only the on-line presentation and thus they do not add new information. One cost here is that it can take more effort to get strangers to agree to link to you than real friends; friends, upon receiving the link request, are likely to say yes (the cost of establishing the relationship has already been paid) whereas a stranger is more likely to refuse such requests. What would make someone agree to link to a complete stranger? One possibility is that they simply want more links—perhaps they are a newcomer to the site and feel conspicuous in the small size of their network or they may be one of the participants who is seeking to build as large a network as they can. Another possibility is that the link seeker has created a particularly intriguing profile and people agree to link to it—or even seek out links with it—because it is so well crafted or features an aesthetic or political viewpoint they wish to espouse. By paying the cost of carefully crafting an interesting profile, one can make more connections. Here we see how the various meanings of a link can be conflated by different participants—a link may be made in response to appreciation of a witty entry, and yet be interpreted as meaning that the linked people know each other.

Furthermore, a connection may know the subject, but not all aspects of his or her personality, work history, etc. Relationships are contextual—a friend known as a supportive shoulder to lean on may not be recognizable as the ruthless poker player or somewhat lax manager he or she also is. Identity is faceted [24]; we have different interests, beliefs, traits, etc., and share different ones with different people. Feld's [10] formulation of how networks form uses the word 'focus' to encompass the different situations, people, ideas, etc., that bring people together. These foci, he pointed out, organise the structure of social networks because they are the circumstances and reasons people meet each other and form ties with each other. The type of information that flows through a tie, whether about the person or about the world at large, depends on the focus that brought them together and on the shared facets of their identity.

The subject's profile may touch upon various facets of his or her identity, and those who are displayed as links may know only some of these. Other claims in the profile may be untrue, yet unquestioned by friends and colleagues, who may simply assume this is an aspect of their acquaintance about which they do not know.

LinkedIn has developed an interesting approach to recognising the focused nature of people's connections. Like several other sites, it includes testimonials, which are comments people write about the subject and which appear alongside the profile and display of connections (see Fig 1 for a sample User Profile page). Unlike links, these need not be reciprocal. They are almost invariably complimentary, since they are displayed at the discretion of the subject (though notions of what is complimentary is quite context dependent). On LinkedIn, these testimonials are situated in specific sections of the profile, rather than as general comments. This is a professional site, aimed at business connections, so the profile sections correspond to different jobs; the testimonials speak about the work the subject did at each work place. The endorsement of one aspect of the profile does not imply any knowledge about the rest. As we will discuss later in this paper, there are a number of reasons for making a self-presentation more faceted; these situated testimonials are a step in that direction.

- Who would impose sanctions

Finally, it is possible that the connections are real people, and they know the subject and know that the profile is deceptive, but they do not care.

Figure 1: Sample Linkedin user profile page.

The culture of the networking sites varies. Some are more playful and participants may see them as an environment for performative expression. On Orkut, a law professor lists his career skills as 'small appliance repair', his career interests as 'large appliance repair'. To those who know him, the joke is obvious. Presented on a site where people often creatively embellish their profiles we can see it not as a deceptive self-description, but as a signal of the author's dry humour.[1] Other sites, such as LinkedIn, are quite business-like and emphasise one's personal responsibility in vouching for another person.

---

1 In fact, Orkut features the category 'sense of humour' as a line in everyone's main profile, with the multiple choice answers including 'obscure', 'clever/quick witted', 'raunchy', etc. Note that this description of one's humour is a conventional signal, with no cost in that domain. Creative and funny use of the profile, however, is a much more reliable signal of one's wit, even as it becomes a less reliable description at face value.

Here, a clearly deceptive statement, such as claiming a higher title at a previous job than was actually held, might indeed be challenged.

3.2 Ensuring co-operation

Yet confrontation is difficult. It is easier to ignore such actions, especially when acting as an individual. But social groups have considerable power in enforcing norms. The power of reputation to enforce co-operative behaviour lies not in confrontation with the subject, but in conversation surrounding him. Displaying connections is a way of signalling a willingness to risk one's reputation. In the real world, as Burt [13] has pointed out, reputation is a powerful force in groups with dense affiliations. This can be due to repeated interactions—we gather a reputation around our identity that, if good, is quite valuable and we benefit from continuing to act in ways that enhance that reputation. But it can also be due to having mutual acquaintances—he cites Granovetter who says that the 'mortification' at having mutual friends discover one's poor behaviour towards another friend is 'unbearable' [25]. A public display of connections, listed along with contact information, arguably provides all viewers of one's network site profile with a virtual set of mutual acquaintances.

> a public display of connections can help someone else establish that they are you

In the pseudonymous dating scene, a frequent complaint is that people act rudely towards each other in ways that they would not do to people they knew in a more integrated social environment. A common complaint concerns dates who break off communication with no explanation, as well as dates who behave boorishly in person. By publicly displaying connections, one provides others with a means of getting in touch with one's circle of friends and acquaintances. One is less likely to treat a date rudely when they are equipped with contact information for many of one's friends. Similarly, poor behaviour is a problem in many on-line discussion forums, where pseudonymity and disconnection provide cover for angry or malicious postings. Several of the social networking sites, such as Orkut and Tribe.net, include user created discussion forums. Here, the participants can be seen in the context of their on-line social network, a context that provides accountability.

The cost of this accountability is a reduction in privacy. The pseudonymous dating sites give people at least the illusion that none of their friends need know how much they would like to find a mate; the pseudonymous forums allow people to express opinions or ask questions on topics that they prefer their acquaintances not know. In the social networking sites, one acts in the company of friends and acquaintances. The security of the named and networked systems comes at the cost of reduced privacy.

The value of the display of connections for ensuring cooperation depends upon the type of connection they represent. If they are vague acquaintances, people known only in the context of the virtual world, there may be little repercussion for poor behaviour, even if the victim complains to the subject's list of contacts. Still, for many people, having bad things said about them, even to distant acquaintances, would be painful and embarrassing. Knowing that everyone they interact with knows of and can communicate with a group of their acquaintances can influence their behaviour. The public display of connections places them in a still virtual, but now public, space.

3.3 Identity theft

The public display of connections can help verify that you are who you say you are. But it can also help someone else establish that they are you, too.

In the face-to-face world, people signal status and seek common ground by selectively divulging information about their own social network.

Name dropping is used to position oneself in a status hierarchy. People may claim connections to celebrities or other high-status people to raise their own status. Here, the goal is not to seek mutual acquaintances but to impress. Such claims to the proximity of fame are often questionable, for once the signaller ascertains that the receiver does not know the famous person he may feel free to make stronger claims of friendship, weaving them with unverifiable yet convincing details.

Name display is also used to discover whether there is a common bond between new acquaintances. People who lived in the same city or attended the same school may go through long lists of names seeking common ground. They find cues about the other's social position in both the lack and presence of mutual acquaintances. There is seldom a question of the veracity of the friendship claims to non-celebrities. If you do not know them, then my claim of friendship with them is meaningless to you and if you do know them, you will be able to easily discover that my claim is false.

Both of these displays of social connection rely on the premise that one's social network is, while not secret, not public either.

John Guare's play 'Six Degrees of Separation' [26], based on the true story of David Hampton [27], is about the power of name-dropping and deceptive display of social network information. The central character is an imposter, Paul, who manoeuvres his way into the lives of several wealthy families with the claim of a close connection to a very famous celebrity and by displaying detailed social network information about their children. Paul says he is the illegitimate son of Sidney Poitier. His listeners cannot directly corroborate or disprove his claim and they end up believing it both because of the wealth of details he supplies, all of which he was able to find in public documents, but also because of their own desire to believe it and to thus have this connection with fame. He becomes even more deeply enmeshed in their lives by saying that he attends Harvard with their children. He knows all their children's names and information about them, and he also knows their children's friends and where they live and what they do; this is what gives him the greatest credibility. It turns out that he had acquired the address book of Trent, a friend of one of the children and had used this normally private information to weave a convincing but deceptive display of what he claimed to be his own network.

Trent had fallen in love with Paul and was coaching him on upper class manners, and offered to provide him with information about all the people in the address book:

> Trent: 'I don't want you to leave me, Paul. I'll go through my address book and tell you about family after family. You'll never not fit in again. We'll give you a new identity. I'll make you the most eagerly sought after young man in the East....

> Trent: Paul stayed with me for three months. We went through the address book letter by letter. Paul vanished by the L's. He took the address book with him ...'

'Six Degrees of Separation' shows the power of social network display. Paul's knowledge of each person was minimal, but he was able to weave a convincing portrait of himself as a member of the group with a few well-chosen details about each.

Participants in social networking sites make this sort of information about their personal social world publicly available—an extensive list of their friends, with a wealth of detail about each individual. Perhaps one day if social network displays become ubiquitous, the signalling value of detailed social network information will decline. But that decline will only occur because the signal loses value through repeated deceptive use. In the meantime, users of on-line social network systems should be aware of the value of the data they are making available on-line—and of the ways that it can potentially be used.

REFERENCES

1. Orkut—http://www.orkut.com/

2. LinkedIn—http://www.linkedin.com/

3. Spoke—http://www.spoke.com/

4. Friendster—http:/www.friendster.com/

5. Wellman B and Potter S: 'The elements of personal community', in Wellman B (Ed): 'Networks in the Global Village', Boulder, CO, Westview Press (1999).

6. Wellman B and Gulia M: 'The network basis of social support: A network is more than the sum of its ties', in Wellman B (Ed): 'Networks in the Global Village', Boulder, CO, Westview Press (1999).

7. Tribe.net—http://www.tribe.net/

8. Ryze—http:/www.ryze.com/

9. boyd d: 'Friendster and publicly articulated social networks', Conference on Human Factors and Computing Systems (CHI 2004), Vienna, ACM (April 2004).

10. Feld S L: 'The focused organisation of social ties', American Journal of Sociology, 86, No 5, pp 1015—1035 (March 1981).

11. Bloch F, Rao V and Desai S: 'Wedding celebrations as conspicuous consumption: signaling social status in rural India', Journal of Human Resources (forthcoming 2004).

12. Csikszentmihályi M and Rochberg H: 'The meaning of things', Cambridge, University of Cambridge Press (1981).

13. Burt R: 'The social capital of structural holes', in Mauro F and Guillén R C, England P and Meyer M (Eds): 'New directions in economic sociology', Russell Sage Foundation (2002).

14. Kim H: 'Social capital, embedded status, and the endorsement effect', Paper prepared for the SSRC workshop on the Corporation as a Social Institution, Institute of Industrial Relations, UC Berkeley (2001).

15. Halle D: 'Inside culture: art and class in American homes', Chicago, University of Chicago Press (1993).

16. Dawkins M S and Guilford T: 'The corruption of honest signalling', Animal Behaviour, 41, pp 865—873 (1991).

17. Grafen A: 'Biological signals as handicaps', Journal of Theoretical Biology, 144, pp 517—546 (1990).

18. Zahavi A: 'The cost of honesty (further remarks on the handicap principle)', Journal of Theoretical Biology, 67, pp 603—605 (1977).

19. Veblen T: 'The theory of the leisure class', New York, Macmillan (1899).

20. Spence M: 'Job market signaling', Quarterly Journal of Economics, 8, pp 355—374 (1973).

21. Donath J: 'Identity and deception in the virtual community', in Kollock P and Smith M (Eds): 'Communities in Cyberspace', Routledge, London (1998).

22. Friedman E J and Resnick P: 'The social cost of cheap pseudonyms', Journal of Economics and Management Strategy 10, No 2, pp 173—199 (2001).

23. Mulrine A: 'Love.com: for better or for worse, the Internet is radically changing the dating scene in America', USA News & World Report (September 2003).

24. boyd d: 'Faceted Id/entity: managing representation in a digital world', MIT Master's Thesis, Cambridge, MA (August 2002).

25. Granovetter M S: 'The strength of weak ties', American Journal of Sociology, 78, pp 1360—1380 (1973).

26. Guare J: 'Six Degrees of Separation', 2nd Ed, New York, Vintage Books (1994).

27. David Hampton Article (July 2003)—http://news.telegraph.co.uk

28. Goffman E: 'The presentation of self in everyday life', New York, Doubleday Anchor (1959).

29. Granovetter M S: 'The strength of weak ties: a network theory revisited', Sociological Theory, 1, pp 201—233 (1983).

30. Lin N: 'Social networks and status attainment', Annual Review of Sociology, 25, pp 467—487 (1999)—http://www.

31. Fischer C: 'America calling', Berkeley, University of California (1992).

Invent

Donath and boyd ask us to consider what individuals learn about each other through their profiles in social networking sites. Choose a profile on a social networking site (it may be your own or that of someone you know, a celebrity or politician, and so on) to look at how this individual has presented his or her personality through this profile. How would you characterize the choices this individual has made to present themselves in a particular way? Then, look at the links—the "public displays of connection." Do the links seem to be to people with similar interests, tastes, and beliefs?

Compose

Choose a photo of yourself that either appears or could appear as a profile picture in a social networking site. Write an essay in which you analyze what your photo says about you to a reader of your profile page. What assumptions might someone make about you based on this photo and why? What does this photo not reveal about you that is important? How might people misinterpret or misunderstand you if all they saw was this photograph in your profile and nothing else?

Collaborate

With your classmates, list the number of connections you have in a particular social networking site (Facebook, LinkedIn, MySpace, Twitter, and so on.). This may range from zero (if you do not have a social networking profile in that site) to hundreds—perhaps thousands! Find out who has the greatest number of connections in a particular site and who has the least. Break these down into strong and weak ties (strong ties are people who are close to you, those who you would consider friends, family, or similar to you, while weak ties are those who are less close to you, such as casual acquaintances and friends of friends). Discuss with each other why some individuals in your group have no online networks, small online networks, large online networks, small or large numbers of weak ties, strong ties, and so on.

(E)DENTITY

What is a friend? What is friendship? Today's social networking sites have challenged our understandings of these terms by labeling every connection as "friend." William Deresiewicz, former associate professor of English at Yale University, paints a picture of historical understandings of friendship to question whether today's social networking connections can truly be considered friends. His article "Faux Friendship" was published in The Chronicle of Higher Education *in December 2009.*

FAUX FRIENDSHIP

By William Deresiewicz

"…[a] numberless multitude of people, of whom no one was close, no one was distant. …"

—*War and Peace*

"Families are gone, and friends are going the same way."

—*In Treatment*

We live at a time when friendship has become both all and nothing at all. Already the characteristically modern relationship, it has in recent decades become the universal one: the form of connection in terms of which all others are understood, against which they are all measured, into which they have all dissolved. Romantic partners refer to each other as boyfriend and girlfriend. Spouses boast that they are each other's best friends. Parents urge their young children and beg their teenage ones to think of them as friends. Adult siblings, released from competition for parental resources that in traditional society made them anything but friends (think of Jacob and Esau), now treat one another in exactly those terms. Teachers, clergymen, and even bosses seek to mitigate and legitimate their authority by asking those they oversee to regard them as friends. We're all on a first-name basis, and when we vote for president, we ask ourselves whom we'd rather have a beer with. As the anthropologist Robert Brain has put it, we're friends with everyone now.

Yet what, in our brave new mediated world, is friendship becoming? The Facebook phenomenon, so sudden and forceful a distortion of social space, needs little elaboration. Having been relegated to our screens, are our friendships now anything more than a form of distraction? When they've shrunk to the size of a wall post, do they retain any content? If we have 768 "friends," in what sense do we have any? Facebook isn't the whole of contemporary friendship, but it sure looks a lot like its future. Yet Facebook—and MySpace, and Twitter, and whatever we're stampeding for next—are just the latest stages of a long attenuation. They've accelerated the fragmentation of consciousness, but they didn't initiate it. They have reified the idea of universal friendship, but they didn't invent it. In retrospect, it seems inevitable that once we decided to become friends with everyone, we would forget how to be friends with anyone. We may pride ourselves today on our aptitude for friendship—friends, after all, are the only people we have left—but it's not clear that we still even know what it means.

How did we come to this pass? The idea of friendship in ancient times could not have been more different. Achilles and Patroclus, David and Jonathan, Virgil's Nisus and Euryalus: Far from being ordinary and universal, friendship, for the ancients, was rare, precious, and hard-won. In a world ordered by relations of kin and kingdom, its elective affinities were exceptional, even subversive, cutting across established lines of allegiance. David loved Jonathan despite the enmity of Saul; Achilles' bond with Patroclus outweighed his loyalty to the Greek cause. Friendship was a high calling, demanding extraordinary qualities of character—rooted in virtue, for Aristotle and Cicero, and dedicated to the pursuit of goodness and truth. And because it was seen as superior to marriage and at least equal in value to sexual love, its expression often reached an erotic intensity. Jonathan's love, David sang, "was more wondrous to me than the love of women." Achilles and Patroclus were not lovers—the men shared a tent, but they shared their beds with concubines—they were something greater. Achilles refused to live without his friend, just as Nisus died to avenge Euryalus, and Damon offered himself in place of Pythias.

The rise of Christianity put the classical ideal in eclipse. Christian thought discouraged intense personal bonds, for the heart should be turned to God. Within monastic communities, particular attachments were seen as threats to group cohesion. In medieval society, friendship entailed specific expectations and obligations, often formalized in oaths. Lords and vassals employed the language of friendship. "Standing surety"—guaranteeing a loan, as in *The Merchant of Venice*—was a chief institution of early modern friendship. Godparenthood functioned in Roman Catholic society (and, in many places, still functions) as a form of alliance between families, a relationship not between godparent and godchild, but godparent and parent. In medieval England, godparents were "godsibs"; in Latin America, they are "compadres," co-fathers, a word we have taken as synonymous with friendship itself.

The classical notion of friendship was revived, along with other ancient modes of feeling, by the Renaissance. Truth and virtue, again, above all: "Those who venture to criticize us perform a remarkable act of friendship," wrote Montaigne, "for to undertake to wound and offend a man for his own good is to have a healthy love for him." His bond with Étienne, he avowed, stood higher not only than marriage and erotic attachment, but also than filial, fraternal, and homosexual love. "So many coincidences are needed to build up such a friendship, that it is a lot if fortune can do it once in three centuries." The highly structured and, as it were, economic nature of medieval friendship explains why true friendship was held to be so rare in classical and neoclassical thought: precisely because relations in traditional societies were dominated by interest. Thus the "true friend" stood against the self-interested "flatterer" or "false friend," as Shakespeare sets Horatio—"more an antique Roman than a Dane"—against Rosencrantz and Guildenstern. Sancho Panza begins as Don Quixote's dependent and ends as his friend; by the close of their journey, he has come to understand that friendship itself has become the reward he was always seeking.

Classical friendship, now called romantic friendship, persisted through the 18th and 19th centuries, giving us the great friendships of Goethe and Schiller, Byron and Shelley, Emerson and Thoreau. Wordsworth addressed his magnum opus to his "dear Friend" Coleridge. Tennyson lamented Hallam—"My friend ... My Arthur ... Dear as the mother to the son"—in the poem that became his masterpiece. Speaking of his first encounter with Hawthorne, Melville was unashamed to write that "a man of deep and noble nature has seized me." But meanwhile, the growth of commercial society was shifting the very grounds of personal life toward the conditions essential for the emergence of modern friendship. Capitalism, said Hume and Smith, by making economic relations impersonal, allowed for private relationships based on nothing other than affection and affinity. We don't know the people who make the things we buy and don't need to know the people who sell them. The ones we do know—neighbors, fellow parishioners, people we knew in high school or college, parents of our children's friends—have no bearing on our economic life. One teaches at a school in the suburbs, another works for a business across town, a third lives on the opposite side of the country. We are nothing to one another but what we choose to become, and we can unbecome it whenever we want.

Add to this the growth of democracy, an ideology of universal equality and inter-involvement. We are citizens now, not subjects, bound together directly rather than through allegiance to a monarch. But what is to bind us emotionally, make us something more than an aggregate of political monads? One answer was nationalism, but another grew out of the 18th-century notion of social sympathy: friendship, or at least, friendliness, as the affective substructure of modern society. It is no accident that "fraternity" made a third with liberty and equality as the watchwords of the French Revolution. Wordsworth in Britain and Whitman in America made visions of universal friendship central to their democratic vistas. For Mary Wollstonecraft, the mother of feminism, friendship was to be the key term of a renegotiated sexual contract, a new domestic democracy.

Now we can see why friendship has become the characteristically modern relationship. Modernity believes in equality, and friendships, unlike traditional relationships, are egalitarian.

Modernity believes in individualism. Friendships serve no public purpose and exist independent of all other bonds. Modernity believes in choice. Friendships, unlike blood ties, are elective; indeed, the rise of friendship coincided with the shift away from arranged marriage. Modernity believes in self-expression. Friends, because we choose them, give us back an image of ourselves.

Modernity believes in freedom. Even modern marriage entails contractual obligations, but friendship involves no fixed commitments. The modern temper runs toward unrestricted fluidity and flexibility, the endless play of possibility, and so is perfectly suited to the informal, improvisational nature of friendship. We can be friends with whomever we want, however we want, for as long as we want.

Social changes play into the question as well. As industrialization uprooted people from extended families and traditional communities and packed them into urban centers, friendship emerged to salve the anonymity and rootlessness of modern life. The process is virtually instinctive now: You graduate from college, move to New York or L.A., and assemble the gang that takes you through your 20s. Only it's not just your 20s anymore. The transformations of family life over the last few decades have made friendship more important still. Between the rise of divorce and the growth of single parenthood, adults in contemporary households often no longer have spouses, let alone a traditional extended family, to turn to for support. Children, let loose by the weakening of parental authority and supervision, spin out of orbit at ever-earlier ages. Both look to friends to replace the older structures. Friends may be "the family we choose," as the modern proverb has it, but for many of us there is no choice but to make our friends our family, since our other families—the ones we come from or the ones we try to start—have fallen apart. When all the marriages are over, friends are the people we come back to. And even those who grow up in a stable family and end up creating another one, pass more and more time between the two. We have yet to find a satisfactory name for that period of life, now typically a decade but often a great deal longer, between the end of adolescence and the making of definitive life choices. But the one thing we know is that friendship is absolutely central to it.

Inevitably, the classical ideal has faded. The image of the one true friend, a soul mate rare to find but dearly beloved, has completely disappeared from our culture. We have our better or lesser friends, even our best friends, but no one in a very long time has talked about friendship the way Montaigne and Tennyson did. That glib neologism "bff," which plays at a lifelong avowal, bespeaks an ironic awareness of the mobility of our connections: Best friends forever may not be on speaking terms by this time next month. We save our fiercest energies for sex. Indeed, between the rise of Freudianism and the contemporaneous emergence of homosexuality to social visibility, we've taught ourselves to shun expressions of intense affection between friends—male friends in particular, though even Oprah was forced to defend her relationship with her closest friend—and have rewritten historical friendships, like Achilles' with Patroclus, as sexual. For all the talk of "bromance" lately (or "man dates"), the term is yet another device to manage the sexual anxiety kicked up by straight-male friendships—whether in the friends themselves or in the people around them—and the typical bromance plot instructs the callow bonds of youth to give way to mature heterosexual relationships. At best, intense friendships are something we're expected to grow out of.

As for the moral content of classical friendship, its commitment to virtue and mutual improvement, that, too, has been lost. We have ceased to believe that a friend's highest purpose is to summon us to the good by offering moral advice and correction. We practice, instead, the nonjudgmental friendship of unconditional acceptance and support—"therapeutic" friendship, in Robert N. Bellah's scornful term. We seem to be terribly fragile now. A friend fulfills her duty, we suppose, by taking our side—validating our feelings, supporting our decisions, helping us to feel good about ourselves. We tell white lies, make excuses when a friend does something wrong, do what we can to keep the boat steady. We're busy people; we want our friendships fun and friction-free.

Yet even as friendship became universal and the classical ideal lost its force, a new kind of idealism arose, a new repository for some of friendship's deepest needs: the group friendship or friendship circle. Companies of superior spirits go back at least as far as Pythagoras and Plato and achieved new importance in the salons and coffeehouses of the 17th and 18th centuries, but the Romantic age gave them a fresh impetus and emphasis. The idea of friendship became central to their self-conception, whether in Wordsworth's circle or the "small band of true friends" who witness Emma's marriage in Austen. And the notion of superiority acquired a utopian cast, so that the circle was seen—not least because of its very emphasis on friendship—as the harbinger of a more advanced age. The same was true, a century later, of the Bloomsbury Group, two of whose members, Woolf and Forster, produced novel upon novel about friendship. It was the latter who famously enunciated the group's political creed. "If I had to choose between betraying my country and betraying my friend," he wrote, "I hope I should have the guts to betray my country." Modernism was the great age of the coterie, and like the legendary friendships of antiquity, modernist friendship circles—bohemian, artistic, transgressive—set their face against existing structures and norms. Friendship becomes, on this account, a kind of alternative society, a refuge from the values of the larger, fallen world.

The belief that the most significant part of an individual's emotional life properly takes place not within the family but within a group of friends began to expand beyond the artistic coterie and become general during the last half of the 20th century. The Romantic-Bloomsburyan prophecy of society as a set of friendship circles was, to a great extent, realized. Mary McCarthy offered an early and tart view of the desirability of such a situation in *The Group*; Barry Levinson, a later, kinder one in *Diner*. Both works remind us that the ubiquity of group friendship owes a great deal to the rise of youth culture. Indeed, modernity associates friendship itself with youth, a time of life it likewise regards as standing apart from false adult values. "The dear peculiar bond of youth," Byron called friendship, inverting the classical belief that its true practice demands maturity and wisdom. With modernity's elevation of youth to supreme status as the most vital and authentic period of life, friendship became the object of intense emotion in two contradictory but often simultaneous directions. We have sought to prolong youth indefinitely by holding fast to our youthful friendships, and we have mourned the loss of youth through an unremitting nostalgia for those friendships. One of the most striking things about the way the 20th century understood friendship was the tendency to view it through the filter of memory, as if it could be recognized only after its loss, and as if that loss were inevitable.

The culture of group friendship reached its apogee in the 1960s. Two of the counterculture's most salient and ideologically charged social forms were the commune—a community of friends in self-imagined retreat from a heartlessly corporatized society—and the rock'n'roll "band" (not "group" or "combo"), its name evoking Shakespeare's "band of brothers" and Robin Hood's band of Merry Men, its great exemplar the Beatles. Communes, bands, and other 60s friendship groups (including Woodstock, the apotheosis of both the commune and the rock concert) were celebrated as joyous, creative places of eternal youth—havens from the adult world. To go through life within one was the era's utopian dream; it is no wonder the Beatles' break-up was received as a generational tragedy. It is also no wonder that 60s group friendship began to generate its own nostalgia as the baby boom began to hit its 30s. *The Big Chill*, in 1983, depicted boomers attempting to recapture the magic of a late-60s friendship circle. ("In a cold world," the movie's tagline reads, "you need your friends to keep you warm.") *Thirtysomething*, taking a step further, certified group friendship as the new adult norm. Most of the characters in those productions, though, were married. It was only in the 1990s that a new generation, remaining single well past 30, found its own images of group friendship in *Seinfeld*, *Sex and the City*, and, of course, *Friends*. By that point, however, the notion of friendship as a redoubt of moral resistance, a shelter from normative pressures and incubator of social ideals, had disappeared. Your friends didn't shield you from the mainstream, they were the mainstream.

And so we return to Facebook. With the social-networking sites of the new century—Friendster and MySpace were launched in 2003, Facebook in 2004—the friendship circle has expanded to engulf the whole of the social world, and in so doing, destroyed both its own nature and that of the individual friendship itself. Facebook's very premise—and promise—is that it makes our friendship circles visible. There they are, my friends, all in the same place. Except, of course, they're not in the same place, or, rather, they're not my friends. They're simulacra of my friends, little dehydrated packets of images and information, no more my friends than a set of baseball cards is the New York Mets.

I remember realizing a few years ago that most of the members of what I thought of as my "circle" didn't actually know one another. One I'd met in graduate school, another at a job, one in Boston, another in Brooklyn, one lived in Minneapolis now, another in Israel, so that I was ultimately able to enumerate some 14 people, none of whom had ever met any of the others. To imagine that they added up to a circle, an embracing and encircling structure, was a belief, I realized, that violated the laws of feeling as well as geometry. They were a set of points, and I was wandering somewhere among them. Facebook seduces us, however, into exactly that illusion, inviting us to believe that by assembling a list, we have conjured a group. Visual juxtaposition creates the mirage of emotional proximity. "It's like they're all having a conversation," a woman I know once said about her Facebook page, full of posts and comments from friends and friends of friends. "Except they're not."

Friendship is devolving, in other words, from a relationship to a feeling—from something people share to something each of us hugs privately to ourselves in the loneliness of our electronic caves, rearranging the tokens of connection like a lonely child playing with dolls. The same path was long ago trodden by community. As the traditional face-to-face community disappeared, we held on to what we had lost—the closeness, the rootedness—by clinging to the word, no matter how much we had to water down its meaning. Now we speak of the Jewish "community" and the medical "community" and the "community" of readers, even though none of them actually is one. What we have, instead of community, is, if we're lucky, a "sense" of community—the feeling without the structure; a private emotion, not a collective experience. And now friendship, which arose to its present importance as a replacement for community, is going the same way. We have "friends," just as we belong to "communities." Scanning my Facebook page gives me, precisely, a "sense" of connection. Not an actual connection, just a sense.

What purpose do all those wall posts and status updates serve? On the first beautiful weekend of spring this year, a friend posted this update from Central Park: "[So-and-so] is in the Park with the rest of the City." The first question that comes to mind is, if you're enjoying a beautiful day in the park, why don't you give your phone a rest? But the more important one is, why did you need to tell us that? We have always shared our little private observations and moments of feeling—it's part of what friendship's about, part of the way we remain present in one another's lives—but things are different now. Until a few years ago, you could share your thoughts with only one friend at a time (on the phone, say), or maybe with a small group, later, in person. And when you did, you were talking to specific people, and you tailored what you said, and how you said it, to who they were—their interests, their personalities, most of all, your degree of mutual intimacy. "Reach out and touch someone" meant someone in particular, someone you were actually thinking about. It meant having a conversation. Now we're just broadcasting our stream of consciousness, live from Central Park, to all 500 of our friends at once, hoping that someone, anyone, will confirm our existence by answering back. We haven't just stopped talking to our friends as individuals, at such moments, we have stopped thinking of them as individuals. We have turned them into an indiscriminate mass, a kind of audience or faceless public. We address ourselves not to a circle, but to a cloud.

It's amazing how fast things have changed. Not only don't we have Wordsworth and Coleridge anymore, we don't even have Jerry and George. Today, Ross and Chandler would be writing on each other's walls. Carrie and the girls would be posting status updates, and if they did manage to find the time for lunch, they'd be too busy checking their BlackBerrys to have a real conversation. *Sex* and *Friends* went off the air just five years ago, and already we live in a different world. Friendship (like activism) has been smoothly integrated into our new electronic lifestyles. We're too busy to spare our friends more time than it takes to send a text. We're too busy, sending texts. And what happens when we do find the time to get together? I asked a woman I know whether her teenage daughters and their friends still have the kind of intense friendships that kids once did. Yes, she said, but they go about them differently. They still stay up talking in their rooms, but they're also online with three other friends, and texting with another three. Video chatting is more intimate, in theory, than speaking on the phone, but not if you're doing it with four people at once. And teenagers are just an early version of the rest of us. A study found that one American in four reported having no close confidants, up from one in 10 in 1985. The figures date from 2004, and there's little doubt that Facebook and texting and all the rest of it have already exacerbated the situation. The more people we know, the lonelier we get.

The new group friendship, already vitiated itself, is cannibalizing our individual friendships as the boundaries between the two blur. The most disturbing thing about Facebook is the extent to which people are willing—are eager—to conduct their private lives in public. "hola cutie-pie! i'm in town on wednesday. lunch?" "Julie, I'm so glad we're back in touch. xoxox." "Sorry for not calling, am going through a tough time right now." Have these people forgotten how to use e-mail, or do they actually prefer to stage the emotional equivalent of a public grope? I can understand "[So-and-so] is in the Park with the rest of the City," but I am incapable of comprehending this kind of exhibitionism. Perhaps I need to surrender the idea that the value of friendship lies precisely in the space of privacy it creates: not the secrets that two people exchange so much as the unique and inviolate world they build up between them, the spider web of shared discovery they spin out, slowly and carefully, together. There's something faintly obscene about performing that intimacy in front of everyone you know, as if its real purpose were to show what a deep person you are. Are we really so hungry for validation? So desperate to prove we have friends?

But surely Facebook has its benefits. Long-lost friends can reconnect, far-flung ones can stay in touch. I wonder, though. Having recently moved across the country, I thought that Facebook would help me feel connected to the friends I'd left behind. But now I find the opposite is true. Reading about the mundane details of their lives, a steady stream of trivia and ephemera, leaves me feeling both empty and unpleasantly full, as if I had just binged on junk food, and precisely because it reminds me of the real sustenance, the real knowledge, we exchange by e-mail or phone or face-to-face. And the whole theatrical quality of the business, the sense that my friends are doing their best to impersonate themselves, only makes it worse. The person I read about, I cannot help feeling, is not quite the person I know.

As for getting back in touch with old friends—yes, when they're people you really love, it's a miracle. But most of the time, they're not. They're someone you knew for a summer in camp, or a midlevel friend from high school. They don't matter to you as individuals anymore, certainly not the individuals they are now, they matter because they made up the texture of your experience at a certain moment in your life, in conjunction with all the other people you knew. Tear them out of that texture—read about their brats, look at pictures of their vacation—and they mean nothing. Tear out enough of them and you ruin the texture itself, replace a matrix of feeling and memory, the deep subsoil of experience, with a spurious sense of familiarity. Your 18-year-old self knows them. Your 40-year-old self should not know them.

Facebook holds out a utopian possibility: What once was lost will now be found. But the heaven of the past is a promised land destroyed in the reaching. Facebook, here, becomes the anti madeleine, an eraser of memory. Carlton Fisk has remarked that he's watched the videotape of his famous World Series home run only a few times, lest it overwrite his own recollection of the event. Proust knew that memory is a skittish creature that peeks from its hole only when it isn't being sought. Mementos, snapshots, reunions, and now this—all of them modes of amnesia, foes of true remembering. The past should stay in the heart, where it belongs.

Finally, the new social-networking Web sites have falsified our understanding of intimacy itself, and with it, our understanding of ourselves. The absurd idea, bruited about in the media, that a MySpace profile or "25 Random Things About Me" can tell us more about someone than even a good friend might be aware of is based on desiccated notions about what knowing another person means: First, that intimacy is confessional—an idea both peculiarly American and peculiarly young, perhaps because both types of people tend to travel among strangers, and so believe in the instant disgorging of the self as the quickest route to familiarity. Second, that identity is reducible to information: the name of your cat, your favorite Beatle, the stupid thing you did in seventh grade. Third, that it is reducible, in particular, to the kind of information that social-networking Web sites are most interested in eliciting, consumer preferences. Forget that we're all conducting market research on ourselves. Far worse is that Facebook amplifies our longstanding tendency to see ourselves ("I'm a Skin Bracer man!") in just those terms. We wear T-shirts that proclaim our brand loyalty, pique ourselves on owning a Mac, and now put up lists of our favorite songs. "15 movies in 15 minutes. Rule: Don't take too long to think about it."

So information replaces experience, as it has throughout our culture. But when I think about my friends, what makes them who they are, and why I love them, it is not the names of their siblings that come to mind, or their fear of spiders. It is their qualities of character. This one's emotional generosity, that one's moral seriousness, the dark humor of a third. Yet even those are just descriptions, and no more specify the individuals uniquely than to say that one has red hair, another is tall. To understand what they really look like, you would have to see a picture. And to understand who they really are, you would have to hear about the things they've done. Character, revealed through action: the two eternal elements of narrative. In order to know people, you have to listen to their stories.

But that is precisely what the Facebook page does not leave room for, or 500 friends, time for. Literally does not leave room for. E-mail, with its rapid-fire etiquette and scrolling format, already trimmed the letter down to a certain acceptable maximum, perhaps a thousand words. Now, with Facebook, the box is shrinking even more, leaving perhaps a third of that length as the conventional limit for a message, far less for a comment. (And we all know the deal on Twitter.) The 10-page missive has gone the way of the buggy whip, soon to be followed, it seems, by the three-hour conversation. Each evolved as a space for telling stories, an act that cannot usefully be accomplished in much less. Posting information is like pornography, a slick, impersonal exhibition. Exchanging stories is like making love: probing, questing, questioning, caressing. It is mutual. It is intimate. It takes patience, devotion, sensitivity, subtlety, skill—and it teaches them all, too.

They call them social-networking sites for a reason. Networking once meant something specific: climbing the jungle gym of professional contacts in order to advance your career. The truth is that Hume and Smith were not completely right. Commercial society did not eliminate the self-interested aspects of making friends and influencing people, it just changed the way we went about it. Now, in the age of the entrepreneurial self, even our closest relationships are being pressed onto this template. A recent book on the sociology of modern science describes a networking event at a West Coast university: "There do not seem to be any singletons—disconsolately lurking at the margins—nor do dyads appear, except fleetingly." No solitude, no friendship, no space for refusal—the exact contemporary paradigm. At the same time, the author assures us, "face time" is valued in this "community" as a "high-bandwidth interaction," offering "unusual capacity for interruption, repair, feedback and learning." Actual human contact, rendered "unusual" and weighed by the values of a systems engineer. We have given our hearts to machines, and now we are turning into machines. The face of friendship in the new century.

In "Faux Friendship," Deresiewicz quotes the anthropologist Robert Brain as saying "We're friends with everyone now." Is the use of the term "friend" in social networking sites problematic for you? Why or why not? What term or terms would you prefer to label your connections in social networking sites?

Deresiewicz historicizes friendship and in many ways romanticizes it. He argues that "the image of the one true friend, a soul mate rare to find but dearly beloved, has completely disappeared from our culture." Based on your experiences and those of others you know, compose a brief essay that responds to Deresiewicz's assertion.

What happens to your email accounts, your social networking profiles, and other elements of your online presence once you die? And what happens if a site like Facebook urges your friends to "reconnect" with you after your death? These issues are ones that online communication sites are more frequently grappling with as their typical users grow older. Jenna Wortham, a staff reporter at the New York Times, investigates ghosts in the social networking machine in her July 2010 New York Times article.

AS FACEBOOK USERS DIE, GHOSTS REACH OUT

BY JENNA WORTHAM

Courtney Purvin got a shock when she visited Facebook last month. The site was suggesting that she get back in touch with an old family friend who played piano at her wedding four years ago.

The friend had died in April.

"It kind of freaked me out a bit," she said. "It was like he was coming back from the dead."

Facebook, the world's biggest social network, knows a lot about its roughly 500 million members. Its software is quick to offer helpful nudges about things like imminent birthdays and friends you have not contacted in a while. But the company has had trouble automating the task of figuring out when one of its users has died.

That can lead to some disturbing or just plain weird moments for Facebook users as the site keeps on shuffling a dead friend through its social algorithms.

Facebook says it has been grappling with how to handle the ghosts in its machine but acknowledges that it has not found a good solution.

"It's a very sensitive topic," said Meredith Chin, a company spokeswoman, "and, of course, seeing deceased friends pop up can be painful." Given the site's size, "and people passing away every day, we're never going to be perfect at catching it," she added.

James E. Katz, a professor of communications at Rutgers University, said the company was experiencing "a coming-of-age problem."

"So many of Facebook's early users were young, and death was rare and unduly tragic," Mr. Katz said.

Now, people over 65 are adopting Facebook at a faster pace than any other age group, with 6.5 million signing up in May alone, three times as many as in May 2009, according to the research firm comScore. People over 65, of course, also have the country's highest mortality rate, so the problem is only going to get worse.

Tamu Townsend, a 37-year-old technical writer in Montreal, said she regularly received prompts to connect with acquaintances and friends who had died.

"Sometimes it's quite comforting when their faces show up," Ms. Townsend said. "But at some point it doesn't become comforting to see that. The service is telling you to reconnect with someone you can't. If it's someone that has passed away recently enough, it smarts."

Ms. Purvin, a 36-year-old teacher living in Plano, Tex., said that after she got over the initial jolt of seeing her friend's face, she was happy for the reminder.

"It made me start talking about him and thinking about him, so that was good," she said.

"But it was definitely a little creepy."

Facebook's approach to the deaths of its users has evolved over time. Early on it would immediately erase the profile of anyone it learned had died.

Ms. Chin says Facebook now recognizes the importance of finding an appropriate way to preserve those pages as a place where the mourning process can be shared online.

Following the Virginia Tech shootings in 2007, members begged the company to allow them to commemorate the victims. Now member profiles can be "memorialized," or converted into tribute pages that are stripped of some personal information and no longer appear in search results. Grieving friends can still post messages on those pages.

Of course, the company still needs to determine whether a user is, in fact, dead. But with a ratio of roughly 350,000 members to every Facebook employee, the company must find ways to let its members and its computers do much of that work.

For a site the size of Facebook, automation is "key to social media success," said Josh Bernoff, an analyst at Forrester Research and co-author of "Groundswell: Winning in a World Transformed by Social Technologies."

"The way to make this work in cases where machines can't make decisions is to tap into the members," he said, pointing to Facebook's buttons that allow users to flag material they find inappropriate. "One way to automate the 'Is he dead' problem is to have a place where people can report it."

That's just what Facebook does. To memorialize a profile, a family member or friend must fill out a form on the site and provide proof of the death, like a link to an obituary or news article, which a staff member at Facebook will then review.

But this option is not well publicized, so many profiles of dead members never are converted to tribute pages. Those people continue to appear on other members' pages as friend suggestions, or in features like the "reconnect" box, which has been spooking the living since it was introduced last October.

Ms. Chin said Facebook was considering using software that would scan for repeated postings of phrases like "Rest in peace" or "I miss you" on a person's page and then dispatch a human to investigate that account.

"We are testing ways to implement software to address this," she said. "But we can't get it wrong. We have to do it correctly."

The scanning approach could invite pranks — as the notification form already has. A friend of Simon Thulbourn, a software engineer living in Germany, found an obituary that mentioned someone with a similar name and submitted it to Facebook last October as evidence that Mr. Thulbourn was dead. He was soon locked out of his own page.

"When I first 'died,' I went looking around Facebook's help pages, but alas, they don't seem to have a 'I'm not really dead, could I have my account back please?' section, so I opted for filling in every form on their Web site," Mr. Thulbourn said by e-mail.

When that didn't work, Mr. Thulbourn created a Web page and posted about it on Twitter until news of the mix-up began to spread on technology blogs and the company took notice. He received an apology from Facebook and got his account back.

The memorializing process has other quirks. Memorial profiles cannot add new friends, so if parents joined the site after a child died, they would not have permission to see all the messages and photos shared by the child's friends.

These are issues that Facebook no doubt wishes it could avoid entirely. But death, of course, is unavoidable, and so Facebook must find a way to integrate it into the social experience online.

"They don't want to be the bearer of bad tidings, but yet they are the keeper of those living memories," Mr. Katz, the Rutgers professor, said. "That's a real downer for a company that wants to be known for social connections and good news."

Invent

While it may seem like a morbid thought, many newspapers and websites create prewritten statements about famous individuals so that, in the case of their death, the site will have a tribute ready to be printed as soon as possible. Examine published eulogies and other tributes to noteworthy individuals and determine what might be a typical style and tone for a eulogy. How would you characterize the composing process for a eulogy or tribute? Would composing in an online space such as Facebook change the process of eulogizing an individual? How and why?

Explore

Choose an online space you frequent—a social networking site, e-mail client, Twitter, online gaming space, etc., and learn more about their policies (if any) for memorializing a user's profile or saving a user's information after death. Would your friends and family members have access to your emails, online profile, and so on after your death? What, if any, measures could you take beforehand to ensure that your information would be accessible to friends and family upon your death?

What would Shakespeare tweet? Given that Shakespeare wrote his plays in the language of his time, would he take to Twitter if he were alive today? Would his tweets be banal ("Just woke up—about to work on a play!") or intriguing? This 2009 USA Today article by reporter Maria Puente asks us to consider "the art of the status update."

WHAT WOULD SHAKESPEARE TWEET?

By Maria Puente

There's an art to writing on Facebook or Twitter, and no one cares that you're 'eating a sandwich'

Not so long ago, people used to keep diaries to record their quotidian doings—privately, of course. Now people keep Facebook and Twitter accounts, updating their status daily, hourly, even minute-by-minute, and almost nothing is private.

Worse, the modern status update is not always compelling reading.

Feeding the cat

Watching TV

Eating a tuna sandwich

To be fair, even great diarists of the past had bad days: Samuel Pepys, the Englishman whose journals clarified a big chunk of the 17th century for historians, sometimes had nothing more imaginative to say than: *And so to bed.*

Surely we could do better 350 years later?

"We all have to go to status-update charm school," jokes Hal Niedzviecki, author of *The Peep Diaries: How We're Learning to Love Watching Ourselves and Our Neighbors*, who joined a slew of online social networks to investigate how they are changing the definition of privacy. "Just one in every million status updates is worth reading, maybe one in every 5 million if you're looking for poetics."

Never mind poetics. Coherence would be nice.

There's no doubt that social-media networks are fantastic communication machines. They allow people to feel connected to a virtual community, make new friends and keep old ones, learn things they didn't know. They encourage people to write more (that can't be bad) and write well and concisely (which is hard, trust us). They are a new form of entertainment (and marketing) that can occupy people for hours in any given day.

"Great blogging is great writing, and it turns out great Twittering is great writing—it's the haiku form of blogging," says Debbie Weil, a consultant on social media and author of *The Corporate Blogging Book*.

But the art of the status update is not much of an art form for millions of people on Facebook, where users can post details of what they're doing for all their friends to see, or on Twitter, where people post tweets about what they're doing that potentially every user can see.

Funny, clever and sassy updates and tweets stand out because they are the exception. Boring, vapid or just TMI—too much information—updates often dominate in cyberspace.

Sheri Peterson, 47, a social worker in Santa Rosa, Calif., is new to Facebook and sometimes can't believe the humdrum nature of what she's reading.

"Some friends—college-educated adults—consistently give lousy updates, such as *Got up; went to store; came home; watched TV*," she says. "Nothing about what kind of store or even what they bought. Was it specialty cheese or incontinence supplies? Nothing about what show they're watching, which could create conversation: '*You like watching Galloping Gourmet reruns? So do I!*' "

Although most of these social-media sites have been around now for at least a few years, it appears many users haven't quite grasped the idea. For some reason, they think their friends and family, plus total strangers, care that they're, say, *Thinking big thoughts*. Yet they don't actually explain those big thoughts and, in the case of Twitter, do it effectively in just 140 characters or less.

"No one cares if you're *On the way to the airport, Checking bags* or *Arrived in Kansas*," says Avery Roth, 23, a public relations coordinator in Dallas. "People who update their status hourly need to cool it. It's also a little vain."

The most inane updates, says Karyn Cronin, 32, an administrative assistant in St. Paul, say things like *Just got back from the grocery store with all the kids, and boy are we exhausted*. "That's just lame," says Cronin, who tries to make her friends laugh by using famous movie lines for her status updates: *Karyn can't handle the truth*, or *Karyn feels a disturbance in the Force*.

Slowly, style and etiquette rules for status updates are evolving, as people get more practice and as skillful updaters become more recognized. There's already a Facebook app called Status King, which allows users to nominate and vote on funny and clever status updates, and buy a T-shirt emblazoned with a favorite. (A recent example: *Suzanne is thinking: Change is inevitable … except from a vending machine*.)

Jeffrey Harmon, 26, of Provo, Utah, and his siblings launched Status King in January and already thousands of updates are posted. (Sample favorite: *Jared is wondering where he's going and why he's in a hand basket*.)

"People spend hours and hours thinking up status updates to win a free T-shirt," Harmon says. He says status updates can be useful for telling friends and family where you are—*Jeff is at Disneyland*—without having to make dozens of phone calls. But because so many people have Twitter and Facebook accounts, information overload can build up and spill over to recipients who don't know Jeff or care that he is at Disneyland.

"The Internet is going through a maturing stage right now," Harmon says. "The only things you should post on Facebook are the things you'd tell your friends in real life. But a lot of people treat it as a personal journal, and they vent. They don't realize they are sharing with all my friends."

When Stephen Stewart, 48, an energy company executive in Sugar Land, Texas, joined Facebook a few months ago, he was shocked when some friends shared private matters in updates.

"One was griping about her bosses—I had to shoot her a private message: 'What are you doing? Delete that comment,'" he says.

So what makes a good status update? "Personality," says Adam Ostrow, editor in chief of Mashable.com, an online publication that covers social networking. "Personality is really what drives people to (follow) you, especially on Twitter."

How to improve your updates? "Follow others who are funny, clear and concise and mimic them, or Twitter a bunch and figure out what people respond to," says Sarah Milstein, co-author of *The Twitter Book*.

Think before you tweet, Ostrow advises. "If this (tweet) were the last thing you ever published, would it be something to be proud of?"

Here's an example of how to improve an update, courtesy of Alison Bailin Batz, 28, a public relations executive in Phoenix and Twitter aficionado: A friend tweets that she just ate some tasty frozen yogurt—and that's it. Why such a useless post? Turns out she was excited because her local frozen yogurt shop was giving away free scoops that day.

"THAT is what (she) should have posted—information that I can use, in this case, free food," Batz says. "We're in the 'whee!' stage of social networking. The trend for 2010 is that everyone is going to cut back, filter, decide whether we really need to follow 1,000 people if they're not interesting. Next year, only the best tweeters survive."

Of course, there is disagreement about what's the best. Milstein argues that even the most banal updates serve a purpose.

"An individual post may not be interesting, but over the course of weeks you build a meaningful picture of somebody, you get a sense of the rhythms of someone's life," she says. Still, "people have to choose to read your updates (on Twitter), and if you're boring, they won't follow you. It's a medium that rewards interestingness."

Interestingness must be in short supply. Anne Trubek, a writer and associate professor of composition and rhetoric at Oberlin College who is studying status updates as a developing 21st-century literary form, sorted them into four categories for her column in the online magazine *GOOD*: The prosaic (*Jill is baking bread*); the informative (*Jack loves this article from GOOD*, followed by the link); the clever and funny (*Johnny thinks Obama should be sworn in a few more times, just to be EXTRA safe*); and the poetic or nonsensical (*If Jim were a cloud, he would rain Earl Grey tea*).

Trubek likes them all, especially for the brevity that forces people to think and write in new ways.

"In the past 10 years, with e-mail and now Facebook and IMing and texting and

Twitter, people feel more connected to writing as a form of expression, and that is wonderful and refreshing," she says.

Indeed, Niedzviecki says, maybe it's just elitism to expect soaring poetry in a status update, when most ordinary people are just looking for a connection they can relate to.

"Most people are not going to have the time or opportunity to find clever links and have interesting things to say 24 hours a day—that's what the celebrities and gurus we follow do, it's their 24-hour job to be entertaining," he says. "For the rest of us, it's, *hey, I just ordered takeout.*

"And that's fine. There's a charm to that."

Choose one of the authors in this textbook and follow them on Twitter if they have an account. How does following an author change the way you interact with their work? Do you receive a different insight into them, their personality, or their writing based on their tweets?

How does the 140 character limit on Twitter constrain an author's ability to write? Does the brevity of a Twitter tweet make you think differently about what you have to say to your social network?

Sign up for a Twitter account and choose a hashtag (a word preceded with a #) to search for at http://search.twitter.com/. For example, if you wanted to see how Twitter users were talking about the results of a recent election, you might search the hashtag #election. After searching for your chosen hashtag and reading the tweets tagged with your chosen word, write a response that analyzes how Twitter users are using this hashtag: What trends do you notice? How do you see an ongoing conversation taking form around this hashtag? What aspects of the conversation are left out or missed because the conversation is taking place via Twitter?

With your classmates, choose an author—Shakespeare or Dr. Seuss, for example— or a fictional character—Mr. Darcy from *Pride and Prejudice* or Juliet from *Romeo and Juliet*, perhaps. Then write a series of tweets from your author or your character in their style of writing or speaking.

U. S. Congresswoman Gabrielle Giffords was shot on January 8, 2011 at a political gathering with her constituents outside of a Safeway grocery store in Tucson, Arizona. After the shooting, online speculation about the motives for the shooting was abundant, especially on Twitter. The following snapshot of a Twitter feed (from January 14, 2011) and news report from Poynter.org show how information, even misinformation, spreads rapidly through the Twitterverse today.

TWITTER WAS AN IMPERFECT NEWS CHANNEL DURING GIFFORDS COVERAGE

By Damon Kiesow

News of the shooting of U.S. Rep. Gabrielle Giffords, was followed quickly by social media receiving more than its share of credit and blame for mistakes made in the early reporting.

But Chad Catacchio at The Next Web writes that Twitter coverage of the event was no better or worse than any individual news anchor:

> "The conflicting reports upset many people, blaming Twitter/ reporters/people sharing the news that they messed up. That, to me, wasn't the case — news organizations were doing their best to get the story as straight as quickly as possible, and many on Twitter were also doing their best to constantly pass on the correct and most up-to-date information. In fact, if anything, it reminded me that news of John F. Kennedy's assassination was handled in quite a similar fashion by [Walter] Cronkite – trying to sort through all of the conflicting reports as an anxious world watched in the real-time of the day."

Dave Wilcox, a PhD student at the University of Wisconsin-Madison School of Journalism & Mass Communication, writes that the coverage on social media points to the need for everyone to be better news consumers as well as producers. He followed events on Twitter and gives the service an "A" for engagement, and a "C-" for accuracy:

"All in all, I believe I would have been far better served as a news consumer if I had simply waited for what my local daily paper put together with their significant resources and skilled editors. But I can't wait; I want my news NOW, damn it. And therein lies a dilemma, of course. To date, we remain far from having old media accuracy at digital media speed."

Steve Safran at Lost Remote chronicles some of the mistakes made, which APPLY NOW included conflicting reports of the congresswoman's death. He asks how media organizations should handle incorrect tweets once the wrong message has already been spread:

"One argument … is to stop or slow the retweeting. But this is difficult, if not impossible. And it is tempting but impractical to call for a squad of people to monitor tweets. For hours after it was reported she was alive, people kept discovering the original tweet that she was dead, retweeting it to their friends without seeing the update. In several cases, the retweet of the incorrect report came three or more hours after the report first spread."

Poynter's Vicki Krueger writes that many newsrooms do not have written policies for the delivery of news over digital channels, and last weekend's events point to a need to address the issue. Krueger writes that an Associated Press Managing Editors study and webinar suggest questions for developing ethics and credibility standards to be applied to Twitter and Facebook messages as well.

 Search

en Globes   Trish Keenan   HappyBDayPeLu   Burgemeester Moerdijk   Kalimba   Ophiuchus

Realtime results for #giffords

3 more tweets since you started searching.

 sfpelosi Changing our words and to set a new tone post-Tucson takes vigilance and consistency. #Giffords #elevatethedebate
less than 20 seconds ago via Twitter for Android

 nubiabennett RT @cnnbrk: Wounded U.S. Rep. #Giffords still in critical condition, continuing to make progress, doctors say. http://on.cnn.com/fNktPw
1 minute ago via web

 lnp_38 RT @WashingtonPost: RT @DavidNakamura: Cell phone of Dr. Peter Rhee, #Giffords doctor, rings during press conference. Ring tone: "Stayin' Alive"
1 minute ago via HootSuite

 TBDNewsTalk Great song to hum during CPR. Perfect beat. MT @DavidNakamura: #Giffords Dr Peter Rhee's cell rings dur. presser. Ring tone: "Stayin' Alive"
2 minutes ago via web

 _rachclark RT @WashingtonPost: RT @DavidNakamura: Cell phone of Dr. Peter Rhee, #Giffords doctor, rings during press conference. Ring tone: "Stayin' Alive"
2 minutes ago via HootSuite

 Solly_Forell NPR Injects Race Into #Giffords Shooting: "A brown #gay saves Congressman fr Gringo's bullets! Truly Sad. . Media: http://soc.li/WnEiv5N
3 minutes ago via Fox News

Solly_Forell NPR Injects Race Into #Giffords Shooting: "A brown #gay saves Congressman fr Gringo's bullets! Truly Sad. . Media: http://soc.li/WnEiv5N

3 minutes ago via Fox News

JoseADelgadoEND RT @WashingtonPost: RT @DavidNakamura: Cell phone of Dr. Peter Rhee, #Giffords doctor, rings during press conference. Ring tone: "Stayin' Alive"

3 minutes ago via HootSuite

MrTerrificPants RT @WashingtonPost: RT @DavidNakamura: Cell phone of Dr. Peter Rhee, #Giffords doctor, rings during press conference. Ring tone: "Stayin' Alive"

3 minutes ago via HootSuite

AmericanPatrol Media excuse #Obama's lies about shootings http://ht.ly/3DZl0 #tcot #giffords #az #arizona #tcot #scumbags #teaparty #tpp #impeach

3 minutes ago via HootSuite

pmnphxaz RT @WashingtonPost: RT @DavidNakamura: Cell phone of Dr. Peter Rhee, #Giffords doctor, rings during press conference. Ring tone: "Stayin' Alive"

4 minutes ago via HootSuite

ctiberius RT @WashingtonPost: RT @DavidNakamura: Cell phone of Dr. Peter Rhee, #Giffords doctor, rings during press conference. Ring tone: "Stayin' Alive"

5 minutes ago via HootSuite

Paolme RT @jocarva: Intolerance breeds intolerance – no matter what religion or race you are (BLOG) http://bit.ly/fmcVyi #iranelection #giffords

5 minutes ago via TweetDeck

joshpolitico I admit, I teared up a bit. - The congresswoman and the astronaut: A love story - http://bit.ly/i5YYpX via @cnn #giffords #kelly

5 minutes ago via web from Skokie, Skokie

Invent

In an age of rapid sharing of information—sometimes misinformation—online, how can we be more careful consumers of information? How can we help avoid the spread of misinformation?

Collaborate

In a small group, compose a list of evaluative criteria that can be applied to information online. How do you know the information is valid? Reliable? Trustworthy? Compare your list of evaluative criteria with your classmates and come up with a compiled list that takes all of the groups' ideas into account.

(E)DENTITY

Malcolm Gladwell, author of The Tipping Point *and* Blink, *argues in this October 2010* New Yorker *piece that because social networks are largely made up of what sociologist Mark Granovetter calls "weak ties," the opportunities for true revolutionary actions in spaces like Twitter or similar social networks are low. Here Gladwell questions how activism might be different in an age of social media.*

SMALL CHANGE
WHY THE REVOLUTION WILL NOT BE TWEETED

By Malcolm Gladwell

At four-thirty in the afternoon on Monday, February 1, 1960, four college students sat down at the lunch counter at the Woolworth's in downtown Greensboro, North Carolina. They were freshmen at North Carolina A.&T., a black college a mile or so away.

"I'd like a cup of coffee, please," one of the four, Ezell Blair, said to the waitress.

"We don't serve Negroes here," she replied.

The Woolworth's lunch counter was a long L-shaped bar that could seat sixty-six people, with a standup snack bar at one end. The seats were for whites. The snack bar was for blacks. Another employee, a black woman who worked at the steam table, approached the students and tried to warn them away. "You're acting stupid, ignorant!" she said. They didn't move. Around five-thirty, the front doors to the store were locked. The four still didn't move. Finally, they left by a side door. Outside, a small crowd had gathered, including a photographer from the Greensboro *Record*. "I'll be back tomorrow with A. & T. College," one of the students said.

Illustration by Seymour Chwast

Social media can't provide what social change has always required.

By next morning, the protest had grown to twenty-seven men and four women, most from the same dormitory as the original four. The men were dressed in suits and ties. The students had brought their schoolwork, and studied as they sat at the counter. On Wednesday, students from Greensboro's "Negro" secondary school, Dudley High, joined in, and the number of protesters swelled to eighty. By Thursday, the protesters numbered three hundred, including three white women, from the Greensboro campus of the University of North Carolina. By Saturday, the sit-in had reached six hundred. People spilled out onto the street. White teenagers waved Confederate flags. Someone threw a firecracker. At noon, the A. & T. football team arrived. "Here comes the wrecking crew," one of the white students shouted.

By the following Monday, sit-ins had spread to Winston-Salem, twenty-five miles away, and Durham, fifty miles away. The day after that, students at Fayetteville State Teachers College and at Johnson C. Smith College, in Charlotte, joined in, followed on Wednesday by students at St. Augustine's College and Shaw University, in Raleigh. On Thursday and Friday, the protest crossed state lines, surfacing in Hampton and Portsmouth, Virginia, in Rock Hill, South Carolina, and in Chattanooga, Tennessee. By the end of the month, there were sit-ins throughout the South, as far west as Texas. "I asked every student I met what the first day of the sitdowns had been like on his campus," the political theorist Michael Walzer wrote in *Dissent*. "The answer was always the same: 'It was like a fever. Everyone wanted to go.'" Some seventy thousand students eventually took part. Thousands were arrested and untold thousands more radicalized. These events in the early sixties became a civil-rights war that engulfed the South for the rest of the decade—and it happened without e-mail, texting, Facebook, or Twitter.

The world, we are told, is in the midst of a revolution. The new tools of social media have reinvented social activism. With Facebook and Twitter and the like, the traditional relationship between political authority and popular will has been upended, making it easier for the powerless to collaborate, coordinate, and give voice to their concerns. When ten thousand protesters took to the streets in Moldova in the spring of 2009 to protest against their country's Communist government, the action was dubbed the Twitter Revolution, because of the means by which the demonstrators had been brought together. A few months after that, when student protests rocked Tehran, the State Department took the unusual step of asking Twitter to suspend scheduled maintenance of its

Web site, because the Administration didn't want such a critical organizing tool out of service at the height of the demonstrations. "Without Twitter the people of Iran would not have felt empowered and confident to stand up for freedom and democracy," Mark Pfeifle, a former national-security adviser, later wrote, calling for Twitter to be nominated for the Nobel Peace Prize. Where activists were once defined by their causes, they are now defined by their tools. Facebook warriors go online to push for change. "You are the best hope for us all," James K. Glassman, a former senior State Department official, told a crowd of cyber activists at a recent conference sponsored by Facebook, A. T. & T., Howcast, MTV, and Google. Sites like Facebook, Glassman said, "give the U.S. a significant competitive advantage over terrorists. Some time ago, I said that Al Qaeda was 'eating our lunch on the Internet.' That is no longer the case. Al Qaeda is stuck in Web 1.0. The Internet is now about interactivity and conversation."

These are strong, and puzzling, claims. Why does it matter who is eating whose lunch on the Internet? Are people who log on to their Facebook page really the best hope for us all? As for Moldova's so-called Twitter Revolution, Evgeny Morozov, a scholar at Stanford who has been the most persistent of digital evangelism's critics, points out that Twitter had scant internal significance in Moldova, a country where very few Twitter accounts exist. Nor does it seem to have been a revolution, not least because the protests—as Anne Applebaum suggested in the *Washington Post*—may well have been a bit of stagecraft cooked up by the government. (In a country paranoid about Romanian revanchism, the protesters flew a Romanian flag over the Parliament building.) In the Iranian case, meanwhile, the people tweeting about the demonstrations were almost all in the West. "It is time to get Twitter's role in the events in Iran right," Golnaz Esfandiari wrote, this past summer, in *Foreign Policy*. "Simply put: There was no Twitter Revolution inside Iran." The cadre of prominent bloggers, like Andrew Sullivan, who championed the role of social media in Iran, Esfandiari continued, misunderstood the situation. "Western journalists who couldn't reach—or didn't bother reaching?—people on the ground in Iran simply scrolled through the English-language tweets post with tag #iranelection," she wrote. "Through it all, no one seemed to wonder why people trying to coordinate protests in Iran would be writing in any language other than Farsi."

Some of this grandiosity is to be expected. Innovators tend to be solipsists. They often want to cram every stray fact and experience into their new model. As the historian Robert Darnton has written, "The marvels of communication technology in the present have produced a false consciousness about the past—even a sense that communication has no history, or had nothing of importance to consider before the days of television and the Internet." But there is something else at work here, in the outsized enthusiasm for social media. Fifty years after one of the most extraordinary episodes of social upheaval in American history, we seem to have forgotten what activism is.

Greensboro in the early nineteen-sixties was the kind of place where racial insubordination was routinely met with violence. The four students who first sat down at the lunch counter were terrified. "I suppose if anyone had come up behind me and yelled 'Boo,' I think I would have fallen off my seat," one of them said later. On the first day, the store manager notified the police chief, who immediately sent two officers to the store. On the third day, a gang of white toughs showed up at the lunch counter and stood ostentatiously behind the protesters, ominously muttering epithets such as "burr-head nigger." A local Ku Klux Klan leader made an appearance. On Saturday, as tensions grew, someone called in a bomb threat, and the entire store had to be evacuated.

The dangers were even clearer in the Mississippi Freedom Summer Project of 1964, another of the sentinel campaigns of the civil-rights movement. The Student Nonviolent Coordinating Committee recruited hundreds of Northern, largely white unpaid volunteers to run Freedom Schools, register black voters, and raise civil-rights awareness in the Deep South. "No one should go *anywhere* alone, but certainly not in an automobile and certainly not at night," they were instructed. Within days of arriving in Mississippi, three volunteers—Michael Schwerner, James Chaney, and Andrew Goodman—were kidnapped and killed, and, during the rest of the summer, thirty-seven black churches were set on fire and dozens of safe houses were bombed; volunteers were beaten, shot at, arrested, and trailed by pickup trucks full of armed men. A quarter of those in the program dropped out. Activism that challenges the status quo—that attacks deeply rooted problems—is not for the faint of heart.

What makes people capable of this kind of activism? The Stanford sociologist Doug McAdam compared the Freedom Summer dropouts with the participants who stayed, and discovered that the key difference wasn't, as might be expected, ideological fervor. "*All* of the applicants—participants and withdrawals alike—emerge as highly committed, articulate supporters of the goals and values of the summer program," he concluded. What mattered more was an applicant's degree of personal connection to the civil-rights movement. All the volunteers were required to provide a list of personal contacts—the people they wanted kept apprised of their activities—and participants were far more likely than dropouts to have close friends who were also going to Mississippi. High-risk activism, McAdam concluded, is a "strong-tie" phenomenon.

This pattern shows up again and again. One study of the Red Brigades, the Italian terrorist group of the nineteen-seventies, found that seventy per cent of recruits had at least one good friend already in the organization. The same is true of the men who joined the mujahideen in Afghanistan. Even revolutionary actions that look spontaneous, like the demonstrations in East Germany that led to the fall of the Berlin Wall, are, at core, strong-tie phenomena. The opposition movement in East Germany consisted of several hundred groups, each with roughly a dozen members.

Each group was in limited contact with the others: at the time, only thirteen percent of East Germans even had a phone. All they knew was that on Monday nights, outside St. Nicholas Church in downtown Leipzig, people gathered to voice their anger at the state. And the primary determinant of who showed up was "critical friends"—the more friends you had who were critical of the regime the more likely you were to join the protest.

So one crucial fact about the four freshmen at the Greensboro lunch counter—David Richmond, Franklin McCain, Ezell Blair, and Joseph McNeil—was their relationship with one another. McNeil was a roommate of Blair's in A. & T.'s Scott Hall dormitory. Richmond roomed with McCain one floor up, and Blair, Richmond, and McCain had all gone to Dudley High School. The four would smuggle beer into the dorm and talk late into the night in Blair and McNeil's room. They would all have remembered the murder of Emmett Till in 1955, the Montgomery bus boycott that same year, and the showdown in Little Rock in 1957. It was McNeil who brought up the idea of a sit-in at Woolworth's. They'd discussed it for nearly a month. Then McNeil came into the dorm room and asked the others if they were ready. There was a pause, and McCain said, in a way that works only with people who talk late into the night with one another, "Are you guys chicken or not?" Ezell Blair worked up the courage the next day to ask for a cup of coffee because he was flanked by his roommate and two good friends from high school.

The kind of activism associated with social media isn't like this at all. The platforms of social media are built around weak ties. Twitter is a way of following (or being followed by) people you may never have met. Facebook is a tool for efficiently managing your acquaintances, for keeping up with the people you would not otherwise be able to stay in touch with. That's why you can have a thousand "friends" on Facebook, as you never could in real life.

This is in many ways a wonderful thing. There is strength in weak ties, as the sociologist Mark Granovetter has observed. Our acquaintances—not our friends—are our greatest source of new ideas and information. The Internet lets us exploit the power of these kinds of distant connections with marvelous efficiency. It's terrific at the diffusion of innovation, interdisciplinary collaboration, seamlessly matching up buyers and sellers, and the logistical functions of the dating world. But weak ties seldom lead to high-risk activism.

In a new book called "The Dragonfly Effect: Quick, Effective, and Powerful Ways to Use Social Media to Drive Social Change," the business consultant Andy Smith and the Stanford Business School professor Jennifer Aaker tell the story of Sameer Bhatia, a young Silicon Valley entrepreneur who came down with acute myelogenous leukemia. It's a perfect illustration of social media's strengths. Bhatia needed a bone-marrow transplant, but he could not find a match among his relatives and friends. The odds were best with a donor of his ethnicity, and there were few South Asians in the national bone-marrow database. So Bhatia's business partner sent out an e-mail explaining Bhatia's plight to more than four hundred of their acquaintances, who forwarded the e-mail to their personal contacts; Facebook pages and YouTube videos were devoted to the Help Sameer campaign. Eventually, nearly twenty-five thousand new people were registered in the bone-marrow database, and Bhatia found a match.

But how did the campaign get so many people to sign up? By not asking too much of them. That's the only way you can get someone you don't really know to do something on your behalf. You can get thousands of people to sign up for a donor registry, because doing so is pretty easy. You have to send in a cheek swab and—in the highly unlikely event that your bone marrow is a good match for someone in need—spend a few hours at the hospital. Donating bone marrow isn't a trivial matter. But it doesn't involve financial or personal risk; it doesn't mean spending a summer being chased by armed men in pickup trucks. It doesn't require that you confront socially entrenched norms and practices. In fact, it's the kind of commitment that will bring only social acknowledgment and praise.

The evangelists of social media don't understand this distinction; they seem to believe that a Facebook friend is the same as a real friend and that signing up for a donor registry in Silicon Valley today is activism in the same sense as sitting at a segregated lunch counter in Greensboro in 1960. "Social networks are particularly effective at increasing motivation," Aaker and Smith write. But that's not true. Social networks are effective at increasing *participation*—by lessening the level of motivation that participation requires. The Facebook page of the Save Darfur Coalition has 1,282,339 members, who have donated an average of nine cents apiece. The next biggest Darfur charity on Facebook has 22,073 members, who have donated an average of thirty-five cents. Help Save Darfur has 2,797 members, who have given, on average, fifteen cents. A spokesperson for the Save Darfur Coalition told *Newsweek*, "We wouldn't necessarily gauge someone's value to the advocacy movement based on what they've given. This is a powerful mechanism to engage this critical population. They inform their community, attend events, volunteer. It's not something you can measure by looking at a ledger." In other words, Facebook activism succeeds not by motivating people to make a real sacrifice, but, by motivating them to do the things that people do when they are not motivated enough to make a real sacrifice. We are a long way from the lunch counters of Greensboro.

The students who joined the sit-ins across the South during the winter of 1960 described the movement as a "fever." But the civil-rights movement was more like a military campaign than like a contagion. In the late nineteen-fifties, there had been sixteen sit-ins in various cities throughout the South, fifteen of which were formally organized by civil-rights organizations like the N.A.A.C.P. and CORE. Possible locations for activism were scouted. Plans were drawn up. Movement activists held training sessions and retreats for would-be protesters. The Greensboro Four were a product of this groundwork: all were members of the N.A.A.C.P. Youth Council. They had close ties with the head of the local N.A.A.C.P. chapter. They had been briefed on the earlier wave of sit-ins in Durham, and had been part of a series of movement meetings in activist churches. When the sit-in movement spread from Greensboro throughout the South, it did not spread indiscriminately. It spread to those cities which had preexisting "movement centers"—a core of dedicated and trained activists ready to turn the "fever" into action.

The civil-rights movement was high-risk activism. It was also, crucially, strategic activism: a challenge to the establishment mounted with precision and discipline.

The N.A.A.C.P. was a centralized organization, run from New York according to highly formalized operating procedures. At the Southern Christian Leadership Conference, Martin Luther King, Jr., was the unquestioned authority. At the center of the movement was the black church, which had, as Aldon D. Morris points out in his superb 1984 study, "The Origins of the Civil Rights Movement," a carefully demarcated division of labor, with various standing committees and disciplined groups. "Each group was task-oriented and coordinated its activities through authority structures," Morris writes. "Individuals were held accountable for their assigned duties, and important conflicts were resolved by the minister, who usually exercised ultimate authority over the congregation."

This is the second crucial distinction between traditional activism and its online variant: social media are not about this kind of hierarchical organization. Facebook and the like are tools for building *networks*, which are the opposite, in structure and character, of hierarchies. Unlike hierarchies, with their rules and procedures, networks aren't controlled by a single central authority. Decisions are made through consensus, and the ties that bind people to the group are loose.

This structure makes networks enormously resilient and adaptable in low-risk situations. Wikipedia is a perfect example. It doesn't have an editor, sitting in New York, who directs and corrects each entry. The effort of putting together each entry is self-organized. If every entry in Wikipedia were to be erased tomorrow, the content would swiftly be restored, because that's what happens when a network of thousands spontaneously devote their time to a task.

There are many things, though, that networks don't do well. Car companies sensibly use a network to organize their hundreds of suppliers, but not to design their cars. No one believes that the articulation of a coherent design philosophy is best handled by a sprawling, leaderless organizational system. Because networks don't have a centralized leadership structure and clear lines of authority, they have real difficulty reaching consensus and setting goals. They can't think strategically; they are chronically prone to conflict and error. How do you make difficult choices about tactics or strategy or philosophical direction when everyone has an equal say?

The Palestine Liberation Organization originated as a network, and the international-relations scholars Mette Eilstrup-Sangiovanni and Calvert Jones argue in a recent essay in *International Security* that this is why it ran into such trouble as it grew: "Structural features typical of networks—the absence of central authority, the unchecked autonomy of rival groups, and the inability to arbitrate quarrels through formal mechanisms—made the P.L.O. excessively vulnerable to outside manipulation and internal strife."

In Germany in the nineteen-seventies, they go on, "the far more unified and successful left-wing terrorists tended to organize hierarchically, with professional management and clear divisions of labor. They were concentrated geographically in universities, where they could establish central leadership, trust, and camaraderie through regular, face-to-face meetings." They seldom betrayed their comrades in arms during police interrogations. Their counterparts on the right were organized as decentralized networks, and had no such discipline. These groups were regularly infiltrated, and members, once arrested, easily gave up their comrades. Similarly, Al Qaeda was most dangerous when it was a unified hierarchy. Now that it has dissipated into a network, it has proved far less effective.

The drawbacks of networks scarcely matter if the network isn't interested in systemic change—if it just wants to frighten or humiliate or make a splash— or if it doesn't need to think strategically. But if you're taking on a powerful and organized establishment you have to be a hierarchy. The Montgomery bus boycott required the participation of tens of thousands of people who depended on public transit to get to and from work each day. It lasted a *year*. In order to persuade those people to stay true to the cause, the boycott's organizers tasked each local black church with maintaining morale, and put together a free alternative private carpool service, with forty-eight dispatchers and forty-two pickup stations. Even the White Citizens Council, King later said, conceded that the carpool system moved with "military precision." By the time King came to Birmingham, for the climactic showdown with Police Commissioner Eugene (Bull) Connor, he had a budget of a million dollars, and a hundred full-time staff members on the ground, divided into operational units. The operation itself was divided into steadily escalating phases, mapped out in advance. Support was maintained through consecutive mass meetings rotating from church to church around the city.

Boycotts and sit-ins and nonviolent confrontations—which were the weapons of choice for the civil-rights movement—are high-risk strategies. They leave little room for conflict and error. The moment even one protester deviates from the script and responds to provocation, the moral legitimacy of the entire protest is compromised. Enthusiasts for social media would no doubt have us believe that King's task in Birmingham would have been made infinitely easier had he been able to communicate with his followers through Facebook, and contented himself with tweets from a Birmingham jail. But networks are messy: think of the ceaseless pattern of correction and revision, amendment and debate, that characterizes Wikipedia. If Martin Luther King, Jr., had tried to do a wiki-boycott in Montgomery, he would have been steamrollered by the white power structure. And of what use would a digital communication tool be in a town where ninety-eight per cent of the black community could be reached every Sunday morning at church? The things that King needed in Birmingham—discipline and strategy—were things that online social media cannot provide.

The bible of the social-media movement is Clay Shirky's "Here Comes Everybody." Shirky, who teaches at New York University, sets out to demonstrate the organizing power of the Internet, and he begins with the story of Evan, who worked on Wall Street, and his friend Ivanna, after she left her smart phone, an expensive Sidekick, on the back seat of a New York City taxicab. The telephone company transferred the data on Ivanna's lost phone to a new phone, whereupon she and Evan discovered that the Sidekick was now in the hands of a teen-ager from Queens, who was using it to take photographs of herself and her friends.

When Evan e-mailed the teen-ager, Sasha, asking for the phone back, she replied that his "white ass" didn't deserve to have it back. Miffed, he set up a Web page with her picture and a description of what had happened. He forwarded the link to his friends, and they forwarded it to their friends. Someone found the MySpace page of Sasha's boyfriend, and a link to it found its way onto the site. Someone found her address online and took a video of her home while driving by; Evan posted the video on the site. The story was picked up by the news filter Digg. Evan was now up to ten e-mails a minute. He created a bulletin board for his readers to share their stories, but it crashed under the weight of responses. Evan and Ivanna went to the police, but the police filed the report under "lost," rather than "stolen," which essentially closed the case. "By this point millions of readers were watching," Shirky writes, "and dozens of mainstream news outlets had covered the story." Bowing to the pressure, the N.Y.P.D. reclassified the item as "stolen." Sasha was arrested, and Evan got his friend's Sidekick back.

Shirky's argument is that this is the kind of thing that could never have happened in the pre-Internet age—and he's right. Evan could never have tracked down Sasha. The story of the Sidekick would never have been publicized. An army of people could never have been assembled to wage this fight. The police wouldn't have bowed to the pressure of a lone person who had misplaced something as trivial as a cell phone. The story, to Shirky, illustrates "the ease and speed with which a group can be mobilized for the right kind of cause" in the Internet age.

Shirky considers this model of activism an upgrade. But it is simply a form of organizing which favors the weak-tie connections that give us access to information over the strong-tie connections that help us persevere in the face of danger. It shifts our energies from organizations that promote strategic and disciplined activity and toward those which promote resilience and adaptability. It makes it easier for activists to express themselves, and harder for that expression to have any impact. The instruments of social media are well suited to making the existing social order more efficient. They are not a natural enemy of the status quo. If you are of the opinion that all the world needs is a little buffing around the edges, this should not trouble you. But if you think that there are still lunch counters out there that need integrating it ought to give you pause.

Shirky ends the story of the lost Sidekick by asking, portentously, "What happens next?"— no doubt imagining future waves of digital protesters. But he has already answered the question. What happens next is more of the same. A networked, weak-tie world is good at things like helping Wall Streeters get phones back from teenage girls. *Viva la revolución.*

Find out more about Mark Granovetter's theories about strong and weak ties. Why does Granovetter say we need both strong and weak ties to function effectively in interpersonal relationships?

Gladwell argues that because social networks are made up largely of weak ties, "real" social activism will never come to pass based on actions performed in social networks. Compose a brief essay that responds to Gladwell's claim by situating it in recent events: Have there been any events of activism or of social change that have emerged from social networks? You may wish to read Jonah Lehrer's *Wired* piece "Weak Ties, Twitter, and Revolution" (http://www.wired.com/wiredscience/2010/09/weak-ties-twitter-and-revolutions/), Biz Stone's *Atlantic* article "Biz Stone on Twitter and Activism" (http://www.theatlantic.com/technology/archive/2010/10/exclusive-biz-stone-on-twitter-andactivism/64772/), or Great Britain's Channel 4 News' article "Arab Revolt: Social Media and the People's Revolution" (http://www.channel4.com/news/arab-revolt-social-media-and-the-peoples-revolution) to inform your response to Gladwell's piece.

Like Gladwell, Nathan Rott looks at online social activism; he asks us to complicate our understandings of home-lessness and advocacy by painting a vivid day-in-the-life of Eric Sheptock, a "homeless homeless advocate" with thousands of friends on Facebook and Twitter. A 2009 graduate of the University of Montana's journalism school, Rott received a Stone & Holt Weeks Fellowship with The Washington Post and National Public Radio. The article that follows was published in the December 13, 2010, issue of The Washington Post.

HOMELESS MAN IN D.C. USES FACEBOOK, SOCIAL MEDIA TO ADVOCATE FOR OTHERS LIKE HIM

By Nathan Rott

Eric Sheptock has 4,548 Facebook friends, 839 Twitter followers, two blogs and an e-mail account with 1,600 unread messages.

What he doesn't have is a place to live.

"I am a homeless homeless advocate," he often tells people. That's the line that hooks them, the one that gives Sheptock—an unemployed former crack addict who hasn't had a permanent address in 15 years—his clout on the issue of homelessness.

His Facebook friends and Twitter followers include policymakers, advocates for the homeless and hundreds of college students who have heard him speak on behalf of the National Coalition for the Homeless.

Being homeless has become Sheptock's full-time occupation. It's work that has provided him with purpose and a sense of community. But it's also work that has perpetuated his homelessness and, in a way, glorified it.

Sheptock, 41, wouldn't take a 9-to-5 job that compromised his advocacy efforts or the long hours he spends tending to his digital empire, he says. He wouldn't move out of the downtown D.C. shelter where he has slept for the past two years if it would make him a less effective voice for change.

"Too many homeless people have come to look up to me, and I can't just walk away from them," he says in a recent blog post titled "Tough Choices." "My conscience won't allow it."

Having 5,000 friends on Facebook is more important to Sheptock than having $5,000 in the bank. And he lives with the consequences of that every day.

'LOTS OF DRAMA'

At 6 a.m., the lights flicker on at the Community for Creative Non-Violence, where Sheptock has occupied the same top bunk since he arrived at the 1,350-bed shelter in 2008.

Eleven other men share a 15-foot-by-18-foot room on a floor that teems with more than 200 people on a typical night. There's not much privacy, Sheptock says. Younger people tend to be loud, older people cranky, and there's drama. "Lots of drama," he says.

That's why, on most days, Sheptock takes a shower as soon as he wakes and then walks the four miles from the shelter near Judiciary Square to Thrive DC, a nonprofit organization in Mount Pleasant where he gets a free breakfast and Internet access. On the days he can afford it, he'll take the bus.

His income varies. November was a good month: He made $330 from his blog posts ($25 a pop at Change.org) and his speeches ($40 for those he gives in the Washington region and $100 for those farther away).

It's not enough to pay rent, he says, "not in this city." But it's enough to pay his cellphone bill and buy the occasional snack or piece of clothing.

Today, he'll take the bus.

PRESSURING CITY OFFICIALS

Breakfast is served at 9:30 a.m. at Thrive DC.

Sheptock, who is wearing a black hooded sweat shirt and cargo pants that hang on his wiry frame, mows through two plates of beenie-weenies, roasted potatoes, coleslaw and bread. He does his laundry and then hustles to Thrive's computer lab, which opens at 11 a.m.

Sheptock is usually there on the dot, says Nathan Mishler, Thrive DC's volunteer resources manager.

"Anyone who deals with homelessness knows of Eric," Mishler says.

Ask city officials about Sheptock, and they'll describe the countless e-mails they've gotten from him complaining about the D.C. government's performance on homelessness.

In a city where 6,500 people have no place to live, affordable housing is scarce and shelters are full, Sheptock "aims to pressure them into actually being effective," his Facebook page says.

His e-mail signature includes his cellphone number, links to his blogs and a slogan: "Outgoing Mayor Fenty has a headache and his headache has a name—Eric Jonathan Sheptock." Then he offers Fenty's office number.

Not everyone appreciates being on the receiving end of Sheptock's constant gripes. One administrator at the Community for Creative Non-Violence says he has marked Sheptock's e-mail as spam because "he's always condemning us for one thing or another."

But others see Sheptock as an important portal to an often voiceless community.

"What he's been great at is surfacing information," says Scott McNeilly of the Washington Legal Clinic for the Homeless. "We have mechanisms in place to respond when there are problems, but often times we don't know that those problems exist."

This year, Sheptock contacted Laura Zeilinger, who oversees the city's homeless services, because of a water leak in the women's shelter at CCNV.

"It's taken the city longer to fix this water leak than it took them to stop the oil leak in the Gulf Coast," he told her.

She quoted him, and within weeks the leak was fixed.

REVOLUTION BY TWEET

Three of Thrive's six computers are in use this morning. A woman mumbles into her cellphone, her long nails clacking against the keyboard as she takes an online typing class. Two men, still bundled in heavy coats, fill out job applications.

Sheptock logs in and finds 27 new Facebook messages and 74 updates but doesn't look at any of them. They are usually event information or group notices, he says.

Instead, he checks his wall, which he has plastered with links to articles about poverty and help for the disadvantaged: the dangers of a proposed residency requirement for D.C. shelters, how to give during the holiday season, a soup kitchen locator.

But no one has commented on anything he has posted.

He goes to his e-mail and discovers 1,601 unread messages in his Yahoo inbox.

"I got it down to about 900 a month ago, but it's shot back up since," he says. "I can't keep up with it."

Most are mass e-mails: newsletters, press releases and spam. One is a public hearing notice from a fellow advocate, which he forwards to other advocates.

"I don't think I'd be able to do much of anything without the Internet," Sheptock says.

After Thrive DC's computer lab closes at 1 p.m., he usually relocates to the Library of Congress or one of the city's public libraries to use their computers.

Most days, Sheptock says, he spends five to six hours online. Social networking, he says, is the key in the battle to make affordable housing a right.

"The tea party started with a tweet, you know," he says.

A HAUNTED CHILDHOOD

It was Facebook that reconnected Sheptock to his family—the people who took him in after he'd been abandoned and probably abused as a baby.

There is much he doesn't know about what happened. He can only point to the long, thin scar on the back of his head and repeat what he was told: He was found in a hotel room in New Jersey at 8 months old, head bleeding, skull fractured.

After three craniotomies and five years of foster care, he was adopted into a strict Pentecostal family, becoming the 10th of what would eventually be 37 Sheptock children. Thirty of the children were adopted like him; many had disabilities.

Although doctors once predicted that Sheptock's head injuries would make it impossible for him to succeed academically or socially, he graduated from high school in 1987.

"He could do so many things very well," says his mother, Joanne Sheptock, 73, who didn't hear from Eric for years. "He could do math like you wouldn't believe" but also was quiet, shy and slower than other kids.

After high school, Sheptock worked as a freight handler and maintenance man before getting into a dispute with his boss and walking off the job. On Feb. 14, 1994, the day before his 25th birthday, he received his last full-time paycheck.

He gradually fell into homelessness and started using crack cocaine—an addiction he conquered, but not before serving multiple stints in jail, including one for 10 months, for possession and other drug-related offenses.

In 2005, he came to the District to protest the war in Iraq and wound up moving into the Franklin School Shelter.

It was there, amid a long-running battle with the city over the shelter's future, that Sheptock began to emerge as an advocate. And it was there that he realized how important it would be to learn to use a computer.

When the Franklin School Shelter closed in 2008, many of its 300 residents were offered transitional apartments. Sheptock was not one of them, he says.

He's okay with that, although people frequently don't understand why.

"I can hear the guy sitting in the living room, saying why doesn't he get off his [butt] and do something, he's doing all of this other stuff," says Neil Donovan, executive director for the National Coalition for the Homeless. "It's not that simple, though," especially not for someone who has been living in shelters as long as Sheptock has.

Studies have found that after six months of homelessness, people undergo a "psychological and sociological change," Donovan says. They stop seeing themselves as a person experiencing homelessness and start seeing themselves as a homeless person. Their situation turns into their identity.

Homelessness, Donovan says, "becomes who you are."

WORK TO DO

Sheptock's hands hover above the keyboard in a pearly white research room at the Library of Congress.

His backward hat bobs to the Arrested Development Pandora Radio station as he focuses on deciphering a fold-creased letter lying next to him.

He is transcribing the scribbled handwriting of a woman who lives at his shelter into a formal request for cleaning supplies so residents can deal with a bedbug infestation. It is signed "Deborah."

She has asked for his help with the letter, he says, because she can't use a computer.

So with his Facebook page and blog open in separate windows—surrounded by his thousands of friends and followers—the homeless homeless advocate types.

In a few hours, Sheptock will return to the shelter, his bunk bed and his 11 roommates. But for now, he has a job to do. He looks comfortable sitting there, legs splayed out, hunched over the keyboard.

He looks at home.

In this piece about homelessness and social networking, Nathan Rott not only shares quotes from his interviews with Eric Sheptock but also cites city officials who know Sheptock: a volunteer resources manager, an administrator at the Community for Creative Non-Violence, and the executive director for the National Coalition for the Homeless. What is the effect Rott creates in his piece by citing these different voices? By including these individuals' reactions to Sheptock, does it make the piece more or less persuasive overall for you?

Using the Internet, find out more about the author of this piece, Nathan Rott, and the newspaper it was written for, The Washington Post. Based on what you learn about Rott and The Washington Post, examine some of the rhetorical choices that the author makes. Why does he write his piece the way he does? How might those rhetorical choices have been different if the article had been written for another newspaper, a magazine, or a blog post?

With a small group of classmates, examine the conversation about social activism in Gladwell's and Rott's articles. Discuss with your group whether you found Gladwell or Rott more persuasive and why. Examine the authors' language choices, style and tone, use of evidence, and use of visual descriptions. Then, list some stylistic choices that could have improved what you consider the less-persuasive article: What would have made this article more convincing for you and your group?

(E)DENTITY

Often controversial, British author Andrew Sullivan has long been a blogger, writing The Daily Dish *(http://andrew-sullivan.theatlantic.com/) since 2000. He explores his avid interest in blogging in this November 2008 piece for* The Atlantic, *considering the intersections between the public and the private inherent in the genre of blogging.*

excerpt from

WHY I BLOG

By Andrew Sullivan

For centuries, writers have experimented with forms that evoke the imperfection of thought, the inconstancy of human affairs, and the chastening passage of time. But as blogging evolves as a literary form, it is generating a new and quintessentially postmodern idiom that's enabling writers to express themselves in ways that have never been seen or understood before. Its truths are provisional, and its ethos collective and messy. Yet the interaction it enables between writer and reader is unprecedented, visceral, and sometimes brutal. And make no mistake: it heralds a golden era for journalism.

The word *blog* is a conflation of two words: *Web* and *log*. It contains in its four letters a concise and accurate self-description: it is a log of thoughts and writing posted publicly on the World Wide Web. In the monosyllabic vernacular of the Internet, *Web log* soon became the word *blog*.

Also see: http://podcasts.theatlantic.com/2008/10/your-brain-on-blog.php

Andrew Sullivan and Marc Ambinder discuss the narcotic appeal of blogging and the occupational hazards of thinking quickly. This form of instant and global self-publishing, made possible by technology widely available only for the past decade or so, allows for no retroactive editing (apart from fixing minor typos or small glitches) and removes from the act of writing any considered or lengthy review. It is the spontaneous expression of instant thought—impermanent beyond even the ephemera of daily journalism. It is accountable in immediate and unavoidable ways to readers and other bloggers, and linked via hypertext to continuously multiplying references and sources. Unlike any single piece of print journalism, its borders are extremely porous and its truth inherently transitory. The consequences of this for the act of writing are still sinking in.

A ship's log owes its name to a small wooden board, often weighted with lead, that was for centuries attached to a line and thrown over the stern. The weight of the log would keep it in the same place in the water, like a provisional anchor, while the ship moved away. By measuring the length of line used up in a set period of time, mariners could calculate the speed of their journey (the rope itself was marked by equidistant "knots" for easy measurement). As a ship's voyage progressed, the course came to be marked down in a book that was called a log.

In journeys at sea that took place before radio or radar or satellites or sonar, these logs were an indispensable source for recording what actually happened. They helped navigators surmise where they were and how far they had traveled and how much longer they had to stay at sea. They provided accountability to a ship's owners and traders. They were designed to be as immune to faking as possible. Away from land, there was usually no reliable corroboration of events apart from the crew's own account in the middle of an expanse of blue and gray and green; and in long journeys, memories always blur and facts disperse. A log provided as accurate an account as could be gleaned in real time.

As you read a log, you have the curious sense of moving backward in time as you move forward in pages—the opposite of a book. As you piece together a narrative that was never intended as one, it seems—and is—more truthful. Logs, in this sense, were a form of human self-correction. They amended for hindsight, for the ways in which human beings order and tidy and construct the story of their lives as they look back on them. Logs require a letting-go of narrative because they do not allow for a knowledge of the ending. So they have plot as well as dramatic irony—the reader will know the ending before the writer did.

Anyone who has blogged his thoughts for an extended time will recognize this world. We bloggers have scant opportunity to collect our thoughts, to wait until events have settled and a clear pattern emerges. We blog now—as news reaches us, as facts emerge. This is partly true for all journalism, which is, as its etymology suggests, daily writing, always subject to subsequent revision. And a good columnist will adjust position and judgment and even political loyalty over time, depending on events. But a blog is not so much daily writing as hourly writing. And with that level of timeliness, the provisionality of every word is even more pressing—and the risk of error or the thrill of prescience that much greater.

No columnist or reporter or novelist will have his minute shifts or constant small contradictions exposed as mercilessly as a blogger's are. A columnist can ignore or duck a subject less noticeably than a blogger committing thoughts to pixels several times a day. A reporter can wait—must wait— until every source has confirmed. A novelist can spend months or years before committing words to the world. For bloggers, the deadline is always now. Blogging is therefore to writing what extreme sports are to athletics: more free-form, more accident-prone, less formal, more alive. It is, in many ways, writing out loud.

You end up writing about yourself, since you are a relatively fixed point in this constant interaction with the ideas and facts of the exterior world. And in this sense, the historic form closest to blogs is the diary. But with this difference: a diary is almost always a private matter. Its raw honesty, its dedication to marking life as it happens and remembering life as it was, makes it a terrestrial log. A few diaries are meant to be read by others, of course, just as correspondence could be—but usually posthumously, or as a way to compile facts for a more considered autobiographical rendering. But a blog, unlike a diary, is instantly public. It transforms this most personal and retrospective of forms into a painfully public and immediate one. It combines the confessional genre with the log form and exposes the author in a manner no author has ever been exposed before.

I remember first grappling with what to put on my blog. It was the spring of 2000 and, like many a freelance writer at the time, I had some vague notion that I needed to have a presence "online." I had no clear idea of what to do, but a friend who ran a Web-design company offered to create a site for me, and, since I was technologically clueless, he also agreed to post various essays and columns as I wrote them. Before too long, this became a chore for him, and he called me one day to say he'd found an online platform that was so simple I could henceforth post all my writing myself. The platform was called Blogger.

As I used it to post columns or links to books or old essays, it occurred to me that I could also post new writing—writing that could even be exclusive to the blog. But what? Like any new form, blogging did not start from nothing. It evolved from various journalistic traditions. In my case, I drew on my mainstream-media experience to navigate the virgin sea. I had a few early inspirations: the old Notebook section of *The New Republic*, a magazine that, under the editorial guidance of Michael Kinsley, had introduced a more English style of crisp, short commentary into what had been a more high-minded genre of American opinion writing. *The New Republic* had also pioneered a Diarist feature on the last page, which was designed to be a more personal, essayistic, first-person form of journalism. Mixing the two genres, I did what I had been trained to do—and improvised.

I'd previously written online as well, contributing to a listserv for gay writers and helping Kinsley initiate a more discursive form of online writing for *Slate*, the first magazine published exclusively on the Web. As soon as I began writing this way, I realized that the online form rewarded a colloquial, unfinished tone. In one of my early Kinsley-guided experiments, he urged me not to think too hard before writing. So I wrote as I'd write an e-mail—with only a mite more circumspection. This is hazardous, of course, as anyone who has ever clicked Send in a fit of anger or hurt will testify. But blogging requires an embrace of such hazards, a willingness to fall off the trapeze rather than fail to make the leap.

From the first few days of using the form, I was hooked. The simple experience of being able to directly broadcast my own words to readers was an exhilarating literary liberation. Unlike the current generation of writers, who have only ever blogged, I knew firsthand what the alternative meant. I'd edited a weekly print magazine, *The New Republic*, for five years, and written countless columns and essays for a variety of traditional outlets. And in all this, I'd often chafed, as most writers do, at the endless delays, revisions, office politics, editorial fights, and last-minute cuts for space that dead-tree publishing entails. Blogging—even to an audience of a few hundred in the early days—was intoxicatingly free in comparison. Like taking a narcotic.

It was obvious from the start that it was revolutionary. Every writer since the printing press has longed for a means to publish himself and reach—instantly— any reader on Earth. Every professional writer has paid some dues waiting for an editor's nod, or enduring a publisher's incompetence, or being ground to literary dust by a legion of fact-checkers and copy editors. If you added up the time a writer once had to spend finding an outlet, impressing editors, sucking up to proprietors, and proofreading edits, you'd find another lifetime buried in the interstices. But with one click of the Publish Now button, all these troubles evaporated.

Alas, as I soon discovered, this sudden freedom from above was immediately replaced by insurrection from below. Within minutes of my posting something, even in the earliest days, readers responded. Email seemed to unleash their inner beast. They were more brutal than any editor, more persnickety than any copy editor, and more emotionally unstable than any colleague.

Again, it's hard to overrate how different this is. Writers can be sensitive, vain souls, requiring gentle nurturing from editors, and oddly susceptible to the blows delivered by reviewers. They survive, for the most part, but the thinness of their skins is legendary. Moreover, before the blogosphere, reporters and columnists were largely shielded from this kind of direct hazing. Yes, letters to the editor would arrive in due course and subscriptions would be canceled. But reporters and columnists tended to operate in a relative sanctuary, answerable mainly to their editors, not readers. For a long time, columns were essentially monologues published to applause, muffled murmurs, silence, or a distant heckle. I'd gotten blowback from pieces before—but in an amorphous, time-delayed, distant way. Now the feedback was instant, personal, and brutal.

And so blogging found its own answer to the defensive counterblast from the journalistic establishment. To the charges of inaccuracy and unprofessionalism, bloggers could point to the fierce, immediate scrutiny of their readers. Unlike newspapers, which would eventually publish corrections in a box of printed spinach far from the original error, bloggers had to walk the walk of self-correction in the same space and in the same format as the original screwup. The form was more accountable, not less, because there is nothing more conducive to professionalism than being publicly humiliated for sloppiness. Of course, a blogger could ignore an error or simply refuse to acknowledge mistakes. But if he persisted, he would be razzed by competitors and assailed by commenters and abandoned by readers. In an era when the traditional media found itself beset by scandals as disparate as Stephen Glass, Jayson Blair, and Dan Rather, bloggers survived the first assault on their worth. In time, in fact, the high standards expected of well-trafficked bloggers spilled over into greater accountability, transparency, and punctiliousness among the media powers that were. Even *New York Times* columnists were forced to admit when they had been wrong.

The blog remained a *superficial* medium, of course. By superficial, I mean simply that blogging rewards brevity and immediacy. No one wants to read a 9,000-word treatise online. On the Web, one-sentence links are as legitimate as thousand-word diatribes—in fact, they are often valued more. And, as Matt Drudge told me when I sought advice from the master in 2001, the key to understanding a blog is to realize that it's a broadcast, not a publication. If it stops moving, it dies. If it stops paddling, it sinks.

But the superficiality masked considerable depth—greater depth, from one perspective, than the traditional media could offer. The reason was a single technological innovation: the hyperlink. An old-school columnist can write 800 brilliant words analyzing or commenting on, say, a new think-tank report or scientific survey. But in reading it on paper, you have to take the columnist's presentation of the material on faith, or be convinced by a brief quotation (which can always be misleading out of context). Online, a hyperlink to the original source transforms the experience. Yes, a few sentences of bloggy spin may not be as satisfying as a full column, but the ability to read the primary material instantly—in as careful or shallow a fashion as you choose—can add much greater context than anything on paper. Even a blogger's chosen pull quote, unlike a columnist's, can be effortlessly checked against the original. Now this innovation, pre-dating blogs but popularized by them, is increasingly central to mainstream journalism.

A blog, therefore, bobs on the surface of the ocean but has its anchorage in waters deeper than those print media is technologically able to exploit. It disempowers the writer to that extent, of course. The blogger can get away with less and afford fewer pretensions of authority. He is—more than any writer of the past—a node among other nodes, connected but unfinished without the links and the comments and the track-backs that make the blogosphere, at its best, a conversation, rather than a production.

A writer fully aware of and at ease with the provisionality of his own work is nothing new. For centuries, writers have experimented with forms that suggest the imperfection of human thought, the inconstancy of human affairs, and the humbling, chastening passage of time. If you compare the meandering, questioning, unresolved dialogues of Plato with the definitive, logical treatises of Aristotle, you see the difference between a skeptic's spirit translated into writing and a spirit that seeks to bring some finality to the argument. Perhaps the greatest single piece of Christian apologetics, Pascal's *Pensées*, is a series of meandering, short, and incomplete stabs at arguments, observations, insights. Their lack of finish is what makes them so compelling—arguably more compelling than a polished treatise by Aquinas.

Or take the brilliant polemics of Karl Kraus, the publisher of and main writer for *Die Fackel*, who delighted in constantly twitting authority with slashing aphorisms and rapid-fire bursts of invective. Kraus had something rare in his day: the financial wherewithal to self-publish. It gave him a fearlessness that is now available to anyone who can afford a computer and an Internet connection.

But perhaps the quintessential blogger *avant la lettre* was Montaigne. His essays were published in three major editions, each one longer and more complex than the previous. A passionate skeptic, Montaigne amended, added to, and amplified the essays for each edition, making them three-dimensional through time. In the best modern translations, each essay is annotated, sentence by sentence, paragraph by paragraph, by small letters (A, B, and C) for each major edition, helping the reader see how each rewrite added to or subverted, emphasized or ironized, the version before. Montaigne was living his skepticism, daring to show how a writer evolves, changes his mind, learns new things, shifts perspectives, grows older—and that this, far from being something that needs to be hidden behind a veneer of unchanging authority, can become a virtue, a new way of looking at the pretensions of authorship and text and truth. Montaigne, for good measure, also peppered his essays with myriads of what bloggers would call external links. His own thoughts are strewn with and complicated by the aphorisms and anecdotes of others. Scholars of the sources note that many of these "money quotes" were deliberately taken out of context, adding layers of irony to writing that was already saturated in empirical doubt.

To blog is therefore to let go of your writing in a way, to hold it at arm's length, open it to scrutiny, allow it to float in the ether for a while, and to let others, as Montaigne did, pivot you toward relative truth. A blogger will notice this almost immediately upon starting. Some e-mailers, unsurprisingly, know more about a subject than the blogger does. They will send links, stories, and facts, challenging the blogger's view of the world, sometimes outright refuting it, but more frequently adding context and nuance and complexity to an idea. The role of a blogger is not to defend against this but to embrace it. He is similar in this way to the host of a dinner party. He can provoke discussion or take a position, even passionately, but he also must create an atmosphere in which others want to participate.

That atmosphere will inevitably be formed by the blogger's personality. The blogosphere may, in fact, be the least veiled of any forum in which a writer dares to express himself. Even the most careful and self-aware blogger will reveal more about himself than he wants to in a few unguarded sentences and that he will be exposed, undone, humiliated—is not available to a blogger. You can't have blogger's block. You have to express yourself now, while your emotions roil, while your temper flares, while your humor lasts. You can try to hide yourself from real scrutiny, and the exposure it demands, but it's hard. And that's what makes blogging as a form stand out: it is rich in personality. The faux intimacy of the Web experience, the closeness of the e-mail and the instant message, seeps through. You feel as if you know bloggers as they go through their lives, experience the same things you are experiencing, and share the moment. When readers of my blog bump into me in person, they invariably address me as Andrew. Print readers don't do that. It's Mr. Sullivan to them.

Explore

Sullivan examines the choices that bloggers make when writing. Choose a popular blog (you could search for one to explore here: http://technorati.com/blogs/top100) and spend some time exploring the blog, reading multiple posts, the "about me" section if one exists, comments on the posts, and so on. After exploring the contents of your chosen blog, write a rhetorical analysis of the site. Who do you believe is the intended audience of this blog and why? How does the author of the blog appeal to his or her readers?

Invent

Trace the history of blogging as a writing activity. When were some of the first blogs written? What are some famous blogs that have emerged over the years? Who came up with the terms "blog" and "blogosphere"?

Compose

Start a blog using a free online service like Blogger (http://www.blogger.com/) or Wordpress (http://wordpress.org/). Choose a name for your blog and think of its story: What purpose will your blog serve? What will you share with your readers? Who do you hope will read your blog? Then, compose your first blog entry. Introduce yourself to your readers and describe what you hope your blog will do. You may even want to link to other blogs you hope to emulate or that have similar themes in what is called your "blog roll."

Elizabeth Kolbert has worked with The New Yorker since 1999, mainly writing on environmentalism. But here, she looks at the propagation of misinformation spread via the World Wide Web: How are rumors started and spread online? In this 2009 article for The New Yorker, Kolbert uses the debate about President Barack Obama's birthplace to frame her discussion about misinformation online.

THE THINGS PEOPLE SAY
RUMORS IN AN AGE OF UNREASON

By Elizabeth Kolbert

This past June, Representative Mike Castle held a town-hall meeting at a community center in Georgetown, Delaware. Castle, a Republican, is the state's only House member, and he had invited half a dozen health-care experts to take questions from his constituents. A woman in a red shirt spent most of the meeting with her hand in the air. When Castle called on her, she rose from her seat, clutching a zip-lock bag filled with papers and a miniature American flag.

"Congressman Castle," she began. "I have a birth certificate here from the United States of America saying I'm an American citizen. With a seal on it. Signed by a doctor. With a hospital administrator's name, my parents, my date of birth, the time, the date. I want to go back to January 20th and I want to know: why are you people ignoring his birth certificate?"

"Yeah!" a man in the audience shouted. The Congressman appeared flummoxed. The health-care experts looked on, impassively.

"He is not an American citizen," the woman in red went on. "He is a citizen of Kenya.

"I am American," she continued. "My father fought in World War Two with the greatest generation in the Pacific theatre." She waved the flag and the zip-lock bag in Castle's direction. "And I don't want this flag to change. I want my country back!" The community center erupted in applause.

The phenomenon known variously as the "birther movement," the "birther conspiracy," and the "birther nut-job fantasy" is now roughly two years old. Its adherents hold that Barack Obama, owing to his birthplace (wherever that may be), is ineligible to be President. As articles of faith go, this one falls somewhere between a belief in Santa Claus and "The Protocols of the Elders of Zion." Obama's birth certificate, which has been posted on the Internet, shows that he was delivered in Honolulu on August 4, 1961, at 7:24 P.M. Further confirmation of these facts exists in the form of birth announcements that appeared in two Honolulu newspapers, the *Advertiser* and the *Star-Bulletin*, the relevant pages of which have also been scanned and posted on the Web. So unambiguous is the evidence that a spokesman for the Republican National Committee has called the question of Obama's birthplace an "unnecessary distraction," and most elected officials have either ignored it or dismissed it as nonsense.

"If you're referring to the President there, he is a citizen of the United States," Representative Castle told the woman in red. (Her response was to lead the crowd in an impromptu recitation of the Pledge of Allegiance.)

Still, the birthers are legion. So far, more than half a dozen lawsuits have been filed alleging that Obama is not a "natural born" citizen. One plaintiff, an Army reservist from Georgia, argued in court that he couldn't be sent to fight in Afghanistan because the military lacked a Commander-in-Chief. In a poll released over the summer, twenty-eight per cent of the Republicans surveyed said that they did not think Obama was born in the U.S., and thirty per cent said that they were unsure, meaning that fully half took birther ideas seriously enough to doubt the legitimacy of their government. When a video of the woman in red was posted on YouTube, it quickly went viral; within a few weeks, it had received some eight hundred thousand hits.

That such a wacky idea should be so persistent is, to put it mildly, disquieting. Here we are, quadrillions of bytes deep into the Information Age. And yet information, it seems, has never mattered less.

According to Cass R. Sunstein, the situation was to be anticipated. Sunstein, who for many years taught at the University of Chicago Law School, recently became the head of the White House Office of Information and Regulatory Affairs. One of the country's most prolific legal scholars—"He seems to write a book about as often as most people run the dishwasher" is how *Esquire* once put it—Sunstein has long been preoccupied with what might be called "virtual civics." He has written four books on this topic—"Republic.com" (2001), "Infotopia" (2006), "Republic.com 2.0" (2007), and, now, "On Rumors: How Falsehoods Spread, Why We Believe Them, What Can Be Done" (Farrar, Straus & Giroux; $18)—all, to varying degrees, dystopic.

Sunstein begins with the relatively uncontroversial premise that a vigorous exchange of information is critical to the democratic process. As he acknowledges, the Web makes virtually unlimited amounts of information available; it is now possible to sit in a coffee shop in New York and read not just the newspapers from Chicago, Boston, and Los Angeles but also those from Cairo, Beijing, and London, while simultaneously receiving e-mail alerts on the latest movie openings and corporate mergers. From this, it is often argued that the Internet is a boon to democracy—if information is good, then more information must be better. But, in Sunstein's view, the Web has a feature that is even more salient: at the same time that it makes more news available, it also makes more news avoidable.

"The most striking power provided by emerging technologies," he has written, is the *"growing power of consumers to 'filter' what they see."* Many of the most popular Web sites are still those belonging to the major news channels and papers—CNN, the BBC, the New York *Times*. Increasingly, though, people are getting information from these sites in a customized form, by subscribing to e-mails and RSS feeds on their favorite topics and skipping subjects they find less congenial. Meanwhile, some of the fastest-growing sites are those which explicitly cater to their users' ideologies. Left-leaning readers know, for example, that if they go to the Huffington Post or to AlterNet they will find stories that support their view of the world. Right-leaning readers know to go to the Drudge Report or to Newsmax to find stories that fit their preconceptions.

And what holds true for the news sites is even more so for the blogosphere, where it's possible to spend hours surfing without ever entering new waters. Conservative blogs like Power Line almost always direct visitors to other conservative blogs, like No Left Turns, while liberal blogs like Daily Kos guide them to others that are also liberal, like Firedoglake. A study of the twenty most-visited blogs in each camp in the months leading up to the 2004 Presidential election found that more than eighty-five per cent of their links were to other blogs with similar politics. When the study's authors charted the links in graphic form, they came up with a picture of non-interaction—a dense scribble on one side, a dense scribble on the other, and only the thinnest strands connecting the two. In 2006, Sunstein performed his own study of fifty political sites. He found that more than four-fifths linked to like-minded sites but only a third linked to sites with an opposing viewpoint. Moreover, many of the links to the opposing side's sites were offered only to illustrate how "dangerous, dumb, or contemptible the views of the adversary really are."

"I do not mean to deny the obvious fact that any system that allows for freedom of choice will create some balkanization of opinion," Sunstein writes, in "Republic.com 2.0." "Long before the advent of the Internet, and in an era of a handful of television stations, people made self-conscious choices among newspapers and radio stations." But, he argues, Web culture takes choice to a new level.

In 1970, two psychologists at a small college in Michigan performed the following experiment. After administering a questionnaire on racial attitudes to seniors at some nearby high schools, they divided the students into groups. Those students who, based on their answers to the questionnaire, exhibited "high prejudice" were placed with others equally biased. Those who expressed "low prejudice" were grouped with those who were similarly tolerant. The students were then instructed to discuss issues like school busing and fair housing. Finally, they were asked to fill out another questionnaire. The surveys revealed a striking pattern: simply by talking to one another, the bigoted students had become more bigoted and the tolerant more tolerant.

People's tendency to become more extreme after speaking with like-minded others has become known as "group polarization," and it has been documented in dozens of other experiments. In one, feminists who spoke with other feminists became more adamant in their feminism. In a second, opponents of same-sex marriage became even more opposed to the idea, while proponents shifted further in favor. In a third, doves who were grouped with other doves became more dovish still. (Interestingly, in this last experiment hawks, after talking to other hawks, became less hawkish, though they remained more hawkish than the doves.) Even judges have been shown to exhibit "group polarization." Democratic appointees who sit with other Democrats are, it's been found, more likely to cast liberal votes than Democratic appointees who sit with Republicans, while Republican appointees on all-Republican panels are more likely to take conservative positions.

Why group polarization occurs is not entirely clear. According to one theory, when people engage in discussions with others who share their opinion they are apt to hear new arguments in favor of it, which prompts them to believe in it all the more strongly. According to a second theory, people are always trying to outdo one another; if everyone in a group agrees that men are jerks, then someone in the group is bound to argue that they're assholes. In ordinary life, there are, of course, many opportunities to engage in group polarization—at the country club, in the union hall, at church or in synagogue, at the monthly meeting of the local feminist book club. Here again, though, Sunstein maintains, the Web takes things to a whole new level.

(Group polarization, it should be noted, is the subject of another recent Sunstein book, "Going to Extremes: How Like Minds Unite and Divide.") There is virtually no opinion an individual can hold that is so outlandish that he will not find other believers on the Web. "Views that would ordinarily dissolve, simply because of an absence of social support, can be found in large numbers on the Internet, even if they are understood to be exotic, indefensible, or bizarre in most communities," Sunstein observes. Racists used to have to leave home to meet up with other racists (or Democrats with other Democrats, or Republicans with Republicans); now they need not even get dressed in order to "chat" with their ideological soul mates.

"It seems plain that the Internet is serving, for many, as a breeding group for extremism, precisely because like-minded people are deliberating with greater ease and frequency with one another," Sunstein writes. He refers to this process as "cyberpolarization."

Put the Web's filtering tools together with cyberpolarization and what you get, by Sunstein's account, are the perfect conditions for spreading misinformation. Who, on liberal blogs, is going to object to (or even recognize) a few misstatements about Sarah Palin? And who, on conservative blogs, is going to challenge mistaken assertions (or, if you prefer, lies) about President Obama?

In the spring of 2008, as the general-election campaign was getting under way, several rumors were circulating about Obama. In addition to the one about his birthplace, there were rumors that he was a Muslim, that he had attended a madrassa in Indonesia, and that he refused to put his hand over his heart when reciting the Pledge of Allegiance. Obama's campaign aides set up a Web site in response, called Fight the Smears. On it, they posted a clip of a CNN story showing the nondenominational school that Obama had attended in Jakarta and a video of Obama leading the U.S. Senate in the Pledge (with his hand over his heart). They also posted a scan of the candidate's birth certificate. "Next time someone talks about Barack's birth certificate, make sure they see this page," the message accompanying the scan read.

If the Web functioned as its boosters maintain—as a "frictionless" source of information—then that posting would have been the end of things. Instead, of course, it was just the beginning. When those who had been "talking about" Obama's birth certificate looked at it on the Web, what they saw was exactly the opposite of what the Obama campaign had intended. Some blogs noted that if the scan of the certificate was enlarged several times a light halo could be seen around each letter. The crosshatched border on the document did not seem to match the cross-hatching on another birth certificate issued in Hawaii around the same time. The scan did not show the raised seal required of an official state document. Nor did it reveal any crease marks. (A real birth certificate would have had to be folded before being sent in the mail.)

"The image is a horrible forgery," a self-described "forensic computer examiner" calling himself Techdude declared on the right-wing blog Atlas Shrugs.

"Enough work has been done by photoshop experts to show that this is not a real document," ClearCase_guy asserted on the conservative Web site Free Republic. "And that begs the question: WHY?"

Apparently still operating under the assumption that people turn to the Web for information, the Obama campaign tried again. It allowed FactCheck.org, a nonpartisan research organization, to inspect the document at the campaign's headquarters, in Chicago.

"FactCheck.org staffers have now seen, touched, examined and photographed the original birth certificate," the group's Web site announced on August 21, 2008. "Our conclusion: Obama was born in the U.S.A. just as he has always said." Nine high-resolution photos accompanied the post, showing the raised seal, as well as a set of creases.

The birthers were unfazed. "I, for one, of course, am not surprised," JM Hanes wrote on the Web site JustOneMinute. "I mean he's had more than two months to find a better forger." Others insisted that the birth certificate was meaningless, since it was just a computer-generated copy of the original handwritten or typed certificate that should have been filed with the state of Hawaii. When, on October 31, 2008, the Hawaiian health director, Chiyome Fukino, issued a statement saying that she had "personally seen and verified that the Hawai'i State Department of Health has Sen. Obama's original birth certificate on record," this evidence, too, was dismissed. At the time of Obama's Inauguration, the following joke was careering around the Web:

CHIEF JUSTICE ROBERTS: Knock, knock.

BARACK OBAMA: Who's there?

CHIEF JUSTICE ROBERTS: Kenya.

BARACK OBAMA: Kenya who?

CHIEF JUSTICE ROBERTS: Kenya show me your birth certificate before you're sworn in?

In July, when the clip of the woman in red went viral, Fukino felt compelled to announce, for a second time, that Obama had a valid birth certificate on file. FactCheck.org reported this development under the heading "The Last Word? We Wish."

Sunstein's theory of the (Dis)Information Age is pointedly nonjudgmental. By his account, the problem is basically structural: certain tendencies of the human mind interact badly with certain features of modern technology, much as certain prescription drugs interact badly with alcohol. Young or old, bigoted or tolerant, liberal or conservative—everyone is equally implicated here, since everyone is predisposed to the same, or at least analogous, mental habits and has access to the same technological tools. But does that really explain contemporary American politics?

The acquisition of knowledge is, as Sunstein points out, a social process: it is shaped by language, by custom, and, since the Enlightenment, by certain widely accepted standards of evidence and rationality. Suppose there is a debate that pits the National Academy of Sciences against a group of armchair meteorologists. Or, let's say there is a disagreement between Sarah Palin on the one side and every major medical and news organization in the country on the other. Whom are you going to believe? There really shouldn't be any contest here, and yet there is. For a great many Americans, global warming is a hoax and "death panels" a reality.

The most plausible explanation for this dark, post-Enlightenment turn is unavailable to Sunstein; so hard is he trying to be nonpartisan that he can't see the nuts for the trees. Several decades ago, a detachment of the American right cut itself loose from reason, and it has been drifting along happily ever since. If the birthers are more evidently kooky than the global-warming "skeptics" or the death-panellers or the supply-siders or the Swift Boat Veterans for Truth, they are, in their fundamental disregard for the facts, actually mainstream. In a telling association, protesters at the anti-Obama rally held in Washington, D.C., on September 12th carried both "Where's the Birth Certificate?" placards and signs mocking climate legislation, as well as posters accusing the President of being a terrorist, a socialist, and a fascist. The historian Richard Hofstadter's description of the far right in the era of Barry Goldwater could apply equally well today: "I call it the paranoid style simply because no other word adequately evokes the qualities of heated exaggeration, suspiciousness, and conspiratorial fantasy that I have in mind."

Ironically enough, Sunstein himself has recently been the object of a right-wing disinformation campaign. As soon as word got out that he was going to be nominated by the Obama Administration to head the Office of Information and Regulatory Affairs, the American Conservative Union set up a Web site on him. It was called stopsunstein.com. The group objected to, among other things, a suggestion that Sunstein had made in a 2004 essay that animals be given legal standing. This (admittedly provocative) proposal was offered in the context of a discussion of how difficult it is to enforce existing laws against animal cruelty. It was quickly caricatured as an invitation to cows and chickens to clog up the dockets.

"Imagine returning from a successful hunting trip . . . only to find out that you've been subpoenaed for killing your prize," one online commentator railed.

"Who knows, maybe Sunstein would have the family of the dead animal serving as witnesses in court!" Holds were placed on Sunstein's nomination by two Republican senators, other distortions of his writings were offered, and, finally, Fox News's Glenn Beck got into the act, exhorting, in a Twitter message to his supporters, "FIND EVERYTHING YOU CAN ON CASS SUNSTEIN." (In an interesting twist on group polarization, some liberal bloggers, who had initially not been keen on Sunstein's nomination, decided at this point that it must be O.K.; as one of them put it, "If Glenn Beck and the other loons are against him, how bad could he be?")

The Web is certainly a transformative technology, just as TV and radio and newspapers once were. There's a temptation, as a result, to confuse the medium with the message, to assume that, because the Internet is being used to produce a certain political effect, it was somehow destined to do so. This account is, in the end, too easy on us (or at least on them). To borrow that old favorite of the right: computers don't spread rumors; people do.

Invent

Kolbert argues that people look only for information online that support the views they already hold, rather than searching more objectively and allowing for dissenting viewpoints. As a result, there is greater intolerance because people simply become more entrenched in their beliefs. What support does Kolbert provide in her article to make her argument? Does her use of evidence and support attempt to discover dissenting viewpoints about her argument, or does it support her already existing views?

Collaborate

Choose a statement that people could agree or disagree with; for example, "Marijuana should be legalized" or "All people are essentially selfish." Before getting together with a small group, rate on a piece of paper how strongly you agree or disagree with the statement. Your instructor will collect the responses and divide you into small groups of people who responded similarly. Have a brief discussion with your group about the statement and how your group feels about it and why. After you have talked with your group, go back to your seat and rate how strongly you agree or disagree with the statement now. Then, as a class, discuss whether your results seem consistent with Kolbert's description of "group polarization" in her article. What can we learn from the idea of group polarization? How can we try to avoid group polarization in online and offline spaces?

The popular webcomic XKCD, written by Randall Munroe, often focuses on internet culture and humor. In this series of two original images, Munroe creates maps of online communities based on data from 2007 and 2010. In the 2007 map, the size of each segment of the map is drawn from the number of users, while the 2010 map argues that "communities rise and fall, and total membership numbers are no longer a good measure of a community's size and health"; thus, the 2010 map uses the overall number of posts or amount of activity to determine the size of a community. Both maps appeared originally on XKCD.com and have been heavily reprinted and discussed in the various communities detailed on the maps.

XKCD

By Randall Munroe

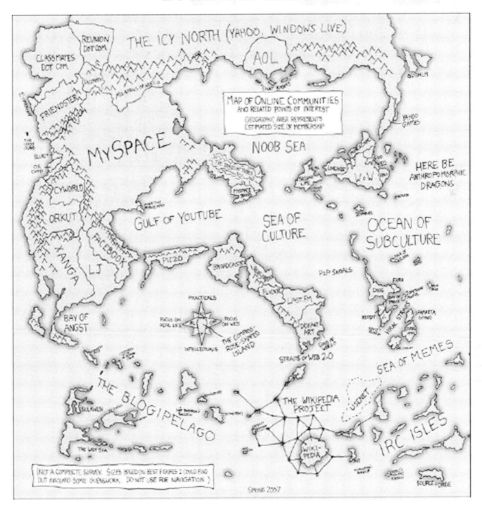

Choose several online communities you are unfamiliar with from the XKCD maps. Navigate to these sites online and discover more about them. Examine their presence on the two maps—has their size, shape, or distribution on the map changed significantly from 2007 to 2010? For example, the social networking site Cyworld has a fairly large portion of the map in 2007, approximately as large as Facebook, but in 2010 Cyworld does not even appear on the map while Facebook has grown to immense proportions—what happened? Why has the map shifted?

Imagine that you are assigned to update the 2010 map once more in 2013. What changes would you make as the cartographer of the online world? What sites are now growing popular that would necessitate a larger portion of the map in 2013? What sites are decreasing in popularity and would be scaled down? What sites are not yet included that should have a new presence on the map in 2013? What sources of data would you consult as you prepare your map and verify its accuracy?

If you had to represent online communities and their rates of socializing and popularity, but could not use a map, what other form might work best and why?

(E)DENTITY

"This is a story about the day Google turned evil," explains science fiction author and blogger Cory Doctorow, co-editor of the blog Boing Boing (chronicling the unusual, interesting, and shocking online). In this fictional story, first published in RadarOnline's October 2007 issue, Google agents question individuals about their search histories and examine possible terrorist connections in their online activities. In the wake of the very real data mining that Google and similar search engines engage in even now, Doctorow wants us to consider whether a future such as this is really science fiction at all.

SCROOGLED

By Cory Doctorow

"Give me six lines written by the most honorable of men, and I will find an excuse in them to hang him." —Cardinal Richelieu

"We don't know enough about you." —Google CEO Eric Schmidt

Greg landed at San Francisco International Airport at 8 p.m., but by the time he'd made it to the front of the customs line, it was after midnight. He'd emerged from first class, brown as a nut, unshaven, and loose-limbed after a month on the beach in Cabo (scuba diving three days a week, seducing French college girls the rest of the time). When he'd left the city a month before, he'd been a stoop-shouldered, potbellied wreck. Now he was a bronze god, drawing admiring glances from the stews at the front of the cabin.

Four hours later in the customs line, he'd slid from god back to man. His slight buzz had worn off, sweat ran down the crack of his ass, and his shoulders and neck were so tense his upper back felt like a tennis racket. The batteries on his iPod had long since died, leaving him with nothing to do except eavesdrop on the middleage couple ahead of him.

"The marvels of modern technology," said the woman, shrugging at a nearby sign: Immigration–Powered by Google.

"I thought that didn't start until next month?" The man was alternately wearing and holding a large sombrero.

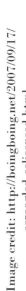

Googling at the border. Christ. Greg had vested out of Google six months before, cashing in his options and "taking some me time"—which turned out to be less rewarding than he'd expected. What he mostly did over the five months that followed was fix his friends' PCs, watch daytime TV, and gain 10 pounds, which he blamed on being at home instead of in the Googleplex, with its well-appointed 24-hour gym.

He should have seen it coming, of course. The U.S. government had lavished $15 billion on a program to fingerprint and photograph visitors at the border, and hadn't caught a single terrorist. Clearly, the public sector was not equipped to Do Search Right.

> The U.S. government had spent $15 billion and hadn't caught a single terrorist. Clearly, the public sector was not equipped to Do Search Right.

The DHS officer had bags under his eyes and squinted at his screen, prodding at his keyboard with sausage fingers. No wonder it was taking four hours to get out of the god damned airport.

"Evening," Greg said, handing the man his sweaty passport. The officer grunted and swiped it, then stared at his screen, tapping. A lot. He had a little bit of dried food at the corner of his mouth and his tongue crept out and licked at it.

"Want to tell me about June 1998?"

Greg looked up from his *Departures*. "I'm sorry?"

"You posted a message to alt.burningman on June 17, 1998, about your plan to attend a festival. You asked, 'Are shrooms really such a bad idea?'"

The interrogator in the secondary screening room was an older man, so skinny he looked like he'd been carved out of wood. His questions went a lot deeper than shrooms.

"Tell me about your hobbies. Are you into model rocketry?"

"What?"

"Model rocketry."

"No," Greg said, "No, I'm not." He sensed where this was going.

The man made a note, did some clicking. "You see, I ask because I see a heavy spike in ads for rocketry supplies showing up alongside your search results and Google mail."

Greg felt a spasm in his guts. "You're looking at my searches and e-mail?" He hadn't touched a keyboard in a month, but he knew what he put into that search bar was likely more revealing than what he told his shrink.

"Sir, calm down, please. No, I'm not looking at your searches," the man said in a mocking whine. "That would be unconstitutional. We see only the ads that show up when you read your mail and do your searching. I have a brochure explaining it. I'll give it to you when we're through here."

"But the ads don't mean anything," Greg sputtered. "I get ads for Ann Coulter ring tones whenever I get e-mail from my friend in Coulter, Iowa!"

The man nodded. "I understand, sir. And that's just why I'm here talking to you. Why do you suppose model rocket ads show up so frequently?"

Greg racked his brain. "Okay, just do this. Search for 'coffee fanatics.'" He'd been very active in the group, helping them build out the site for their coffee-of-the-month subscription service.

The blend they were going to launch with was called Jet Fuel. "Jet Fuel" and "Launch"—that would probably make Google barf up some model rocket ads.

They were in the home stretch when the carved man found the Halloween photos. They were buried three screens deep in the search results for "Greg Lupinski."

"It was a Gulf War–themed party," he said. "In the Castro."

"And you're dressed as...?"

"A suicide bomber," he replied sheepishly. Just saying the words made him wince.

"Come with me, Mr. Lupinski," the man said.

By the time he was released, it was past 3 a.m. His suitcases stood forlornly by the baggage carousel. He picked them up and saw they had been opened and carelessly closed. Clothes stuck out from around the edges.

When he returned home, he discovered that all of his fake pre-Columbian statues had been broken, and his brand-new white cotton Mexican shirt had an ominous boot print in the middle of it. His clothes no longer smelled of Mexico. They smelled like airport.

He wasn't going to sleep. No way. He needed to talk about this. There was only one person who would get it. Luckily, she was usually awake around this hour.

Maya had started working at Google two years after Greg had. It was she who'd convinced him to go to Mexico after he cashed out: Anywhere, she'd said, that he could reboot his existence.

Maya had two giant chocolate labs and a very, very patient girlfriend named Laurie who'd put up with anything except being dragged around Dolores Park at 6 a.m. by 350 pounds of drooling canine.

Maya reached for her Mace as Greg jogged toward her, then did a double take and threw her arms open, dropping the leashes and trapping them under her sneaker. "Where's the rest of you? Dude, you look hot!"

He hugged her back, suddenly conscious of the way he smelled after a night of invasive Googling. "Maya," he said, "What do you know about Google and the DHS?"

She stiffened as soon as he asked the question. One of the dogs began to whine. She looked around, then nodded up at the tennis courts. "Top of the light pole there; don't look," she said. "That's one of our mini WiFi access points. Wide-angle webcam. Face away from it when you talk."

In the grand scheme of things, it hadn't cost Google much to wire the city with webcams. Especially when measured against the ability to serve ads to people based on where they were sitting.

Greg hadn't paid much attention when the cameras on all those access points went public—there'd been a day's worth of blogstorm while people played with the new all-seeing toy, zooming in on various prostitute cruising areas, but after a while the excitement blew over.

Feeling silly, Greg mumbled, "You're joking."

"Come with me," she said, turning away from the pole.

The dogs weren't happy about cutting their walk short, and expressed their displeasure in the kitchen as Maya made coffee.

"We brokered a compromise with the DHS," she said, reaching for the milk. "They agreed to stop fishing through our search records, and we agreed to let them see what ads got displayed for users."

Greg felt sick. "Why? Don't tell me Yahoo was doing it already..."

"No, no. Well, yes. Sure. Yahoo was doing it. But that wasn't the reason Google went along. You know, Republicans hate Google. We're overwhelmingly registered Democratic, so we're doing what we can to make peace with them before they clobber us. This isn't P.I.I."—Personally Identifying Information, the toxic smog of the information age—"It's just metadata. So it's only slightly evil."

"Why all the intrigue, then?"

Maya sighed and hugged the lab that was butting her knee with its huge head. "The spooks are like lice. They get everywhere. They show up at our meetings. It's like being in some Soviet ministry. And the security clearance—we're divided into these two camps: the cleared and the suspect. We all know who isn't cleared, but no one knows why. I'm cleared. Lucky for me, being a dyke no longer disqualifies you. No cleared person would deign to eat lunch with an unclearable."

Greg felt very tired. "So I guess I'm lucky I got out of the airport alive. I might have ended up 'disappeared' if it had gone badly, huh?"

Maya stared at him intently. He waited for an answer.

"What?"

"I'm about to tell you something, but you can't ever repeat it, okay?"

"Um...you're not in a terrorist cell, are you?"

"Nothing so simple. Here's the deal: Airport DHS scrutiny is a gating function. It lets the spooks narrow down their search criteria. Once you get pulled aside for secondary at the border, you become a 'person of interest'—and they never, ever let up. They'll scan webcams for your face and gait. Read your mail. Monitor your searches."

"I thought you said the courts wouldn't let them..."

"The courts won't let them indiscriminately Google you. But after you're in the system, it becomes a selective search. All legal. And once they start Googling you, they always find something. All your data is fed into a big hopper that checks for 'suspicious patterns,' using deviation from statistical norms to nail you."

Greg felt like he was going to throw up. "How the hell did this happen? Google was a good place. 'Don't be evil,' right?" That was the corporate motto, and for Greg, it had been a huge part of why he'd taken his computer science Ph.D. from Stanford directly to Mountain View.

Maya replied with a hard-edged laugh. "Don't be evil? Come on, Greg. Our lobbying group is that same bunch of crypto-fascists that tried to Swift-Boat Kerry. We popped our evil cherry a long time ago."

They were quiet for a minute.

"It started in China," she went on, finally. "Once we moved our servers onto the mainland, they went under Chinese jurisdiction."

Greg sighed. He knew Google's reach all too well: Every time you visited a page with Google ads on it, or used Google maps or Google mail—even if you sent mail to a Gmail account—the company diligently collected your info. Recently, the site's search-optimization software had begun using the data to tailor Web searches to individual users. It proved to be a revolutionary tool for advertisers. An authoritarian government would have other purposes in mind.

> Every time you visited a page with Google ads, or used Google maps, or Google mail—even if you sent mail to a Gmail account—they collected your info.

"They were using us to build profiles of people," she went on. "When they had someone they wanted to arrest, they'd come to us and find a reason to bust them. There's hardly anything you can do on the Net that isn't illegal in China."

Greg shook his head. "Why did they have to put the servers in China?"

"The government said they'd block us otherwise. And Yahoo was there." They both made faces. Somewhere along the way, employees at Google had become obsessed with Yahoo, more concerned with what the competition was doing than how their own company was performing. "So we did it. But a lot of us didn't like the idea."

Maya sipped her coffee and lowered her voice. One of her dogs sniffed insistently under Greg's chair.

"Almost immediately, the Chinese asked us to start censoring search results," Maya said. "Google agreed. The company line was hilarious: 'We're not doing evil—we're giving consumers access to a better search tool! If we showed them search results they couldn't get to, that would just frustrate them. It would be a *bad user experience.*'"

"Now what?" Greg pushed a dog away from him. Maya looked hurt.

"Now you're a person of interest, Greg. You're Googlestalked. Now you live your life with someone constantly looking over your shoulder. You know the mission statement, right? 'Organize the World's Information.' Everything. Give it five years, we'll know how many turds were in the bowl before you flushed. Combine that with automated suspicion of anyone who matches a statistical picture of a bad guy and you're—"

"Scroogled."

"Totally." She nodded.

Maya took both labs down the hall to the bedroom. He heard a muffled argument with her girlfriend, and she came back alone.

"I can fix this," she said in an urgent whisper. "After the Chinese started rounding up people, my podmates and I made it our 20 percent project to fuck with them." (Among Google's business innovations was a rule that required every employee to devote 20 percent of his or her time to high-minded pet projects.) "We call it the Googlecleaner. It goes deep into the database and statistically normalizes you. Your searches, your Gmail histograms, your browsing patterns. All of it. Greg, I can Googleclean you. It's the only way."

"I don't want you to get into trouble."

She shook her head. "I'm already doomed. Every day since I built the damn thing has been borrowed time—now it's just a matter of waiting for someone to point out my expertise and history to the DHS and, oh, I don't know. Whatever it is they do to people like me in the war on abstract nouns."

Greg remembered the airport. The search. His shirt, the boot print in the middle of it.

"Do it," he said.

The Googlecleaner worked wonders. Greg could tell by the ads that popped up alongside his searches, ads clearly meant for someone else: Intelligent Design Facts, Online Seminary Degree, Terror Free Tomorrow, Porn Blocker Software, the Homosexual Agenda, Cheap Toby Keith Tickets. This was Maya's program at work. Clearly Google's new personalized search had him pegged as someone else entirely, a God-fearing right winger with a thing for hat acts.

Which was fine by him.

Then he clicked on his address book, and found that half of his contacts were missing. His Gmail in-box was hollowed out like a termite-ridden stump. His Orkut profile, normalized. His calendar, family photos, bookmarks: all empty. He hadn't quite realized before how much of him had migrated onto the Web and worked its way into Google's server farms—his entire online identity. Maya had scrubbed him to a high gloss; he'd become the invisible man.

Greg sleepily mashed the keys on the laptop next to his bed, bringing the screen to life. He squinted at the flashing toolbar clock: 4:13 a.m.! Christ, who was pounding on his door at this hour?

He shouted, "Coming!" in a muzzy voice and pulled on a robe and slippers. He shuffled down the hallway, turning on lights as he went. At the door, he squinted through the peephole to find Maya staring glumly back at him.

He undid the chains and dead bolt and yanked the door open.

Maya rushed in past him, followed by the dogs and her girlfriend.

She was sheened in sweat, her usually combed hair clinging in clumps to her forehead. She rubbed at her eyes, which were red and lined.

"Pack a bag," she croaked hoarsely.

"What?"

She took him by the shoulders. "Do it," she said.

"Where do you want to...?"

"Mexico, probably. Don't know yet. Pack, dammit." She pushed past him into his bedroom and started yanking open drawers.

"Maya," he said sharply, "I'm not going anywhere until you tell me what's going on."

She glared at him and pushed her hair away from her face. "The Googlecleaner lives. After I cleaned you, I shut it down and walked away. It was too dangerous to use anymore. But it's still set to send me e-mail confirmations whenever it runs. Someone's used it six times to scrub three very specific accounts—all of which happen to belong to members of the Senate Commerce Committee up for reelection."

"Googlers are blackwashing senators?"

"Not Googlers. This is coming from off-site. The IP block is registered in D.C. And the IPs are all used by Gmail users. Guess who the accounts belong to?"

"You spied on Gmail accounts?"

"Okay. Yes. I did look through their e-mail. Everyone does it, now and again, and for a lot worse reasons than I did. But check it out—turns out all this activity is being directed by our lobbying firm. Just doing their job, defending the company's interests."

Greg felt his pulse beating in his temples. "We should tell someone."

"It won't do any good. They know everything about us. They can see every search. Every e-mail. Every time we've been caught on the webcams. Who is in our social network...did you know if you have 15 Orkut buddies, it's statistically certain that you're no more than three steps to someone who's contributed money to a 'terrorist' cause? Remember the airport? You'll be in for a lot more of that."

"Maya," Greg said, getting his bearings. "Isn't heading to Mexico overreacting? Just quit. We can do a start-up or something. This is crazy."

"They came to see me today," she said. "Two of the political officers from DHS. They didn't leave for hours. And they asked me a lot of very heavy questions."

"About the Googlecleaner?"

"About my friends and family. My search history. My personal history."

"Jesus."

"They were sending a message to me. They're watching every click and every search. It's time to go. Time to get out of range."

"There's a Google office in Mexico, you know."

"We've got to go," she said, firmly.

"Laurie, what do you think of this?" Greg asked.

Laurie thumped the dogs between the shoulders. "My parents left East Germany in '65. They used to tell me about the Stasi. The secret police would put everything about you in your file, if you told an unpatriotic joke, whatever. Whether they meant it or not, what Google has created is no different."

"Greg, are you coming?"

He looked at the dogs and shook his head. "I've got some pesos left over," he said. "You take them. Be careful, okay?"

Maya looked like she was going to slug him. Softening, she gave him a ferocious hug.

"Be careful, yourself," she whispered in his ear.

They came for him a week later. At home, in the middle of the night, just as he'd imagined they would.

Two men arrived on his doorstep shortly after 2 a.m. One stood silently by the door. The other was a smiler, short and rumpled, in a sport coat with a stain on one lapel and a American flag on the other. "Greg Lupinski, we have reason to believe you're in violation of the Computer Fraud and Abuse Act," he said, by way of introduction. "Specifically, exceeding authorized access, and by means of such conduct having obtained information. Ten years for a first offense. Turns out that what you and your friend did to your Google records qualifies as a felony. And oh, what will come out in the trial...all the stuff you whitewashed out of your profile, for starters."

Greg had played this scene in his head for a week. He'd planned all kinds of brave things to say. It had given him something to do while he waited to hear from Maya. She never called.

"I'd like to get in touch with a lawyer," is all he mustered.

"You can do that," the small man said. "But maybe we can come to a better arrangement."

Greg found his voice. "I'd like to see your badge," he stammered.

The man's basset-hound face lit up as he let out a bemused chuckle. "Buddy, I'm not a cop," he replied. "I'm a consultant. Google hired me—my firm represents their interests in Washington—to build relationships. Of course, we wouldn't get the police involved without talking to you first. You're part of the family. Actually, there's an offer I'd like to make."

Greg turned to the coffeemaker, dumped the old filter.

"I'll go to the press," he said.

The man nodded as if thinking it over. "Well, sure. You could walk into the *Chronicle*'s office in the morning and spill everything. They'd look for a confirming source. They won't find one. And when they try searching for it, we'll find them. So, buddy, why don't you hear me out, okay? I'm in the win-win business. I'm very good at it." He paused. "By the way, those are excellent beans, but you want to give them a little rinse first? Takes some of the bitterness out and brings up the oils. Here, pass me a colander?"

> The Stasi put everything about you in a file. Whether they meant to or not, what Google did is no different.

Greg watched as the man silently took off his jacket and hung it over a kitchen chair, then undid his cuffs and carefully rolled them up, slipping a cheap digital watch into his pocket. He poured the beans out of the grinder and into Greg's colander, and rinsed them in the sink.

He was a little pudgy and very pale, with the social grace of an electrical engineer. He seemed like a real Googler, actually, obsessed with the minutiae. He knew his way around a coffee grinder, too.

"We're drafting a team for Building 49..."

"There is no Building 49," Greg said automatically.

"Of course," the guy said, flashing a tight smile. "There's no Building 49. But we're putting together a team to revamp the Googlecleaner. Maya's code wasn't very efficient, you know. It's full of bugs. We need an upgrade. You'd be the right guy, and it wouldn't matter what you knew if you were back inside."

"Unbelievable," Greg said, laughing. "If you think I'm going to help you smear political candidates in exchange for favors, you're crazier than I thought."

"Greg," the man said, "we're not smearing anyone. We're just going to clean things up a bit. For some select people. You know what I mean? Everyone's Google profile is a little scary under close inspection. Close inspection is the order of the day in politics. Standing for office is like a public colonoscopy." He loaded the cafetière and depressed the plunger, his face screwed up in solemn concentration. Greg retrieved two coffee cups—Google mugs, of course—and passed them over.

"We're going to do for our friends what Maya did for you. Just a little cleanup.

All we want to do is preserve their privacy. That's all."

Greg sipped his coffee. "What happens to the candidates you don't clean?"

"Yeah," the guy said, flashing Greg a weak grin. "Yeah, you're right. It'll be kind of tough for them." He searched the inside pocket of his jacket and produced several folded sheets of paper. He smoothed out the pages and put them on the table. "Here's one of the good guys who needs our help." It was a printout of a search history belonging to a candidate whose campaign Greg had contributed to in the past three elections.

"Fella gets back to his hotel room after a brutal day of campaigning door to door, fires up his laptop, and types 'hot asses' into his search bar. Big deal, right? The way we see it, for that to disqualify a good man from continuing to serve his country is just un-American."

Greg nodded slowly.

"So you'll help the guy out?" the man asked.

"Yes."

"Good. There's one more thing. We need you to help us find Maya. She didn't understand our goals at all, and now she seems to have flown the coop. Once she hears us out, I have no doubt she'll come around."

He glanced at the candidate's search history.

"I guess she might," Greg replied.

The new Congress took 11 working days to pass the Securing and Enumerating America's Communications and Hypertext Act, which authorized the DHS and NSA to outsource up to 80 percent of intelligence and analysis work to private contractors. Theoretically, the contracts were open to competitive bidding, but within the secure confines of Google's Building 49, there was no question of who would win. If Google had spent $15 billion on a program to catch bad guys at the border, you can bet they would have caught them—governments just aren't equipped to Do Search Right.

The next morning Greg scrutinized himself carefully as he shaved (the security minders didn't like hacker stubble and weren't shy about telling him so), realizing that today was his first day as a de facto intelligence agent for the U.S.

government. How bad would it be? Wasn't it better to have Google doing this stuff than some ham-fisted DHS desk jockey?

By the time he parked at the Googleplex, among the hybrid cars and bulging bike racks, he had convinced himself. He was mulling over which organic smoothie to order at the canteen when his key card failed to open the door to Building 49. The red LED flashed dumbly every time he swiped his card. Any other building, and there'd be someone to tailgate on, people trickling in and out all day. But the Googlers in 49 only emerged for meals, and sometimes not even that.

Swipe, swipe, swipe. Suddenly he heard a voice at his side. Greg, can I see you, please?"

The rumpled man put an arm around his shoulders, and Greg smelled his citrusy aftershave. It smelled like what his dive-master in Baja had worn when they went out to the bars in the evening. Greg couldn't remember his name. Juan Carlos? Juan Luis?

The man's arm around his shoulders was firm, steering him away from the door, out onto the immaculate lawn, past the herb garden outside the kitchen. "We're giving you a couple of days off," he said.

Greg felt a sudden stab of anxiety. "Why?" Had he done something wrong? Was he going to jail?

"It's Maya." The man turned him around, met his eyes with his bottomless gaze. "She killed herself. In Guatemala. I'm sorry, Greg."

Greg seemed to hurtle away, to a place miles above, a Google Earth view of the Googleplex, where he looked down on himself and the rumpled man as a pair of dots, two pixels, tiny and insignificant. He willed himself to tear at his hair, to drop to his knees and weep.

From a long way away, he heard himself say, "I don't need any time off. I'm okay."

From a long way away, he heard the rumpled man insist.

The argument persisted for a long time, and then the two pixels moved into Building 49, and the door swung shut behind them.

Doctorow's fictional story relies on real-life practices to give it a sense of verisimilitude. Research Google's data mining and privacy practices and the USA PATRIOT Act to discover more about the facts that "Scroogled" draws on to create its fictional world.

Write a brief criminal profile in the style and voice of the Homeland Security agents from "Scroogled" based on your search history in Google or a similar search engine as well as your e-mails and other Internet activities. You are the subject—how will you be profiled? What does your online history say about you and your interests? How might your online history be misinterpreted? Would you be Scroogled based on your activities online?

(E)DENTITY

Sherry Turkle has examined the intersections of technology and the self since the late 1970s. In her recent book Alone Together: Why We Expect More from Technology and Less from Each Other, *published in January 2011, she questions whether online communication brings us together in the same ways as offline communications. Perhaps her most famous book,* Life on the Screen: Identity in the Age of the Internet, *considers how online interactions shape our offline lives. Her article "Always-On/Always-On-You" in the 2008 edited collection* Handbook of Mobile Communication Studies *examines cell phones and other devices we carry close to our bodies, asking us to consider whether they are tethered to us or vice versa.*

excerpts from

ALWAYS-ON/ALWAYS-ON-YOU: THE TETHERED SELF

By Sherry Turkle

In the mid-1990s, a group of young researchers at the MIT Media Lab carried computers and radio transmitters in their backpacks, keyboards in their pockets, and digital displays embedded in their eyeglass frames.[1] Always on the Internet, they called themselves "cyborgs." The cyborgs seemed at a remove from their bodies. When their burdensome technology cut into their skin, causing lesions and then scar tissue, they were indifferent. When their encumbrances led them to be taken for the physically disabled, they patiently provided explanations.

---

1   I have studied relational artifacts in the lives of children and the elderly since 1997, beginning with the simple Tamagotchis that were available at every toy store to Kismet and Cog, advanced robots at the MIT Artificial Intelligence Laboratory, and Paro, a seal-like creature designed specifically for therapeutic purposes. Along the way there have been Furbies, AIBOS, and My Real Babies, the latter a baby doll that like the Paro has changing inner states that respond to the quality of its human care. Over 250 subjects have been involved in these studies. My investigations of computer-mediated communication date from the mid-1980s and have followed the media from e-mail, primitive virtual communities, and Web-based chat to cell technology, instant messaging, and social networking. Over 400 subjects have been involved in these studies. My work was done in Boston and Cambridge and their surrounding suburbs. The work on robotics investigated children and seniors from a range of ethnicities and social classes. This was possible because in every case I was providing robots and other relational artifacts to my informants. In the case of the work on communications technology, I spoke to people, children, adolescents, and adults, who already had computers, Web access, mobile phones, BlackBerries, etc. This necessarily makes my claim about their lives in the always-on/always-on-you culture not necessarily generalizable outside of the social class currently wealthy enough to afford such things. This essay expands on themes explored in previous writing. Portions of this essay appeared in Turkle (2006b, 2006c).

They were learning to walk and talk as new creatures, learning to inhabit their own bodies all over again, and yet in a way, they were fading away, bleeding out onto the Net. Their experiment has both a re-embodiment, a prosthetic consummation, and a disembodiment: a disappearance of their bodies into still-nascent computational spaces.

Within a few years, the cyborgs had a new identity as the Media Lab's "Wearable Computing Group." What had been novel in their practice was institutionally reduced to the cyborgs as harbingers of the "cool" clothing of embedded technologies while the rest of us clumsily juggled cell phones, laptops, and PDAs. But the legacy of the MIT cyborgs goes beyond the idea that communications technologies might be wearable (or totable). Core elements of their experience have become generalized in global culture: the experience of living on the net, newly free in some ways, newly yoked in others.

Today, the near-ubiquity of handheld and palm-size computing and cellular technologies that enable voice communication, text-messaging, e-mail, and web access have made connectivity a commonplace. When digital technologies first came onto the consumer market in the form of personal computers, they were objects for personal projection. Computers – in large part because they were programmable, plastic, customizable – came to be experienced as a "second self" (Turkle, 2005a). In the early 21st century, such language does not go far enough; our new intimacy with machines compels us to speak of a new state of the self, itself.

A NEW STATE OF THE SELF, ITSELF

For the most part, our everyday language for talking about technology's effects assumes a life both on and off the screen; it assumes the existence of separate worlds, plugged and unplugged. But some of today's locations suggest a new placement of the subject, such as when we say, "I'll be on my cell," by which we mean "You can reach me; my cell phone will be on, and I am wired into (social) existence through it." *On* my cell, *online*, *on* the web, *on* instant messaging – these phrases suggest a new place for the situation of a *tethered* self.

We are tethered to our "always-on/always-on-us" communications devices and the people and things we reach through them: people, web pages, voice-mail, games, artificial intelligences (non-player game characters, interactive online "bots"). These very different objects achieve a certain sameness because of the way we reach them. Animate and inanimate, they live for us through our tethering devices, always ready-to-mind and hand. The self, now attached to its devices, occupies a liminal space between the physical real and its lives on the screen (Turner, 1969). It participates in both realms at the same time. I once described the rapid movements from physical to a multiplicity of digital selves through the metaphor of "cycling-through." With cell technology, rapid cycling stabilizes into a sense of continual co-presence (Turkle, 1995).

For example, in the past, I did not usually perform my roles as mother in the presence of my professional colleagues. Now a call from my fifteen-year-old daughter calls me forth as a mother. The presence of the cell phone to which only my daughter has the number keeps me alert to its ring all day. Wherever I am, whatever I am doing, I am psychologically tuned to my access to the connections that matter.

THE CONNECTIONS THAT MATTER

We are witnessing a new form of sociality in which the isolation of our physical bodies does not indicate a lack of connectedness but may be its precondition. The connectedness that "matters" is determined by our distance from available communications technology. Increasingly, what people want out of public spaces is that they offer a place to be private with tethering technologies. When everyone is using the devices that connect them to what most "matters," a neighborhood walk reveals a world of madmen and women, talking to themselves, sometimes shouting to themselves, little concerned with what is around them, happy to have intimate conversations in public spaces. In fact, the spaces themselves become liminal, not entirely public, not entirely private.

In a café, a traditionally public space, one learned to lean in toward the person with whom one was speaking, lending an ear while veiling the gaze to better share it with one's interlocutor. Tethering has retrained the body. A hand motion (a finger placed in the ear not at the phone to better wall off the sounds of physical reality) signals an identity shift. On a cell call, the speaker often stares straight ahead, face exposed. He or she talks out loud, behaving as though no one around is listening.

A train station is no longer a communal space, but a space of social collection: tethered selves come together, but do not speak to each other. Each person at the station is more likely to be having an encounter with someone miles away than with the person in the next chair. Each inhabits a private media bubble.

Our media signal that we do not want to be disturbed by conventional sociality with physically proximate individuals.

When people have personal cell phone conversations in public spaces, what sustains their sense of intimacy is the presumption that those around them treat them not only as anonymous, but as close to disembodied. When an individual holds a cell phone (or "speaks into the air," indicating a cell with earphone microphone) they are marked with a certain absence. They are transported to the space of the new ether, virtualized. That sense of "transport" can be signaled in other ways: when one looks down to one's lap at a meal or meeting, the change of gaze has come to signify a glance towards a BlackBerry or other small communications device. The change of gaze is not read as daydreaming, but says that one is focused on other connections. The accessibility of these connections influences our ideas about travel and new experience.

The director of a program that places American students in Greek universities complains that they are not "experiencing Greece" because they spend too much time online, talking with their friends from home. I am sympathetic as she speaks, thinking of the hours I spent walking with my fifteen-year-old daughter on a visit to Paris as she "texts" her friends at home on her cell phone. I worry that she is missing an experience that I cherished in my youth, the experience of an undiluted Paris that came with the thrill of disconnection from where I was from. But she is happy and tells me that keeping in touch is "comforting" and that beyond this, her text mails to home constitute a "diary." She can look back at her texts and remember her state of mind at different points of her trip. Her notes back to friends, translated from instant message shorthand include: "Saw Pont D'Avignon." "Saw World Cup Soccer in Paris." "Went to Bordeaux." It is hard to get in too many words on the phone keyboard and there is no cultural incentive to do so. A friend calls my daughter as we prepare for dinner at our Paris hotel and asks her to lunch in Boston. She says, quite simply: "Not possible, but how about Friday." When I grew up the idea of the "global village" was an abstraction. My daughter lives it on her cell phone. Emotionally, socially, she has not left her life in Boston.

Of course, balancing (and sometimes ignoring) one's physical companions in favor of tethered connections is not limited to those on holiday. Contemporary professional life is rich in examples of people ignoring those they are "with" to give priority to online others who they consider a more relevant audience. Several scenes have become iconic: sessions at international conferences where experts from all over the world do their e-mail; the communications channels that are set up by audience members at conferences to comment on speakers' presentations during the presentations themselves (these conversations are as much about jockeying for professional position among the audience as they are about what is being said at the podium). Here, the presentation becomes a portal to discussions that take people away from it, discussions that tend to take place in hierarchical tiers – only certain people are invited to participate in certain discussions. As a member of the audience, one develops a certain anxiety: have I been invited to chat in the inner circle? Presenters of course, develop their own anxieties. They know that flipped open screens signal that they are at best sharing the audience's attention. And yet, when speakers take their seats in the audience, they, too, flip open their computers to do their e-mail. When an audience member closes down his or her screen, the gesture is a kind of "curtsy," a sign of respect to speakers whose status makes it unseemly to multitask during their presentations.

Observing e-mail and electronic messaging during conferences at exotic locations compels our attention because it is easy to measure the time and money it takes to get everyone physically together at such meetings. Other scenes have become so mundane that we scarcely notice them: students do e-mail during classes; business people do e-mail during meetings; parents do e-mail while talking with their children; couples do e-mail at dinner in restaurants; people talk on the phone and do their e-mail at the same time. Once done surreptitiously, the habit of co-presence is becoming increasingly normalized. Indeed, being "elsewhere" than where you might be has become something of a market of one's sense of self-importance. [...]

[...] LEAVING THE TIME TO TAKE OUR TIME

Always-on/always-on-you communications devices are seductive for many reasons, among them, they give the sense that one can do more, be in more places, control more aspects of life. Those who are attached to BlackBerry technology speak about the fascination of watching their lives "scroll by," of watching their lives as though watching a movie. One develops a new view of self when one considers the many thousands of people to whom one may be connected. Yet just as teenagers may suffer from a media environment that invites them to greater dependency, adults, too, may suffer from being overly tethered, too connected.

We are learning a communications style in which we are accustomed to receiving a hasty message to which we are expected to give a rapid response. Our experience raises the question: are we leaving enough time to take our time?

Adults use tethering technologies during what most of us think of as "down time," the time they might have daydreamed during a cab ride, or while waiting in line or walking to work. This may be time that we physiologically and emotionally need to maintain or restore our ability to focus (Herzog et al., 1997; Kaplan, 1995). Tethering takes time from other activities (particularly those that demand undivided attention), it adds new tasks that take up time (keeping up with e-mail and messages), and adds a new kind of time to the day, the time of attention sharing, sometimes referred to as "continuous partial attention." In all of this, we make our attention into our rarest resource, creating increasingly stiff competition for its deployment, *but we undervalue it as well*. We deny the importance of giving it to one thing and one thing only. [...]

[...] BOUNDARIES

A new complaint in family and business life is that it is hard to know when one has the attention of a BlackBerry user. A parent, partner, or child can be lost for a few seconds or a few minutes to an alternate reality. The shift of attention can be subtle, friends and family are sometimes not aware of the loss until the person has "returned." Indeed, BlackBerry users may not even know where their attention lies. They report that their sense of self has merged with their prosthetic extensions and some see this as a new "high." But this exhilaration may be denying the costs of multitasking. Sociologists who study the boundaries between work and the rest of life suggest that it is helpful when people demarcate role shifts between the two. Their work suggests that being able to use a BlackBerry to blur the line is problematic rather than a skill to be celebrated. (Clark, 2000; Desrochers and Sargent, 2003; Shumate and Fulk, 2004). And celebrating the integration of remote communications into the flow of life may be underestimating the importance of face-to-face connections.

Attention-sharing creates work environments fraught with new tensions over the lack of primacy given to physical proximity. Face-to-face conversations are routinely interrupted by cell phone calls and e-mail reading. Fifteen years ago, if a colleague read mail in your presence, it was considered rude. These days, turning away from the person in front of you to answer a cell phone has become the norm. Additionally, for generations, business people have grown accustomed to relying on time in taxis, airports, trains and limos to get to know each other and to discuss substantive matters. The waiting time in client outer offices was precious time for work and the exchange of news that created social bonds among professional colleagues. Now, things have changed: professionals spend taxi time on their cell phones or doing e-mail on their BlackBerries. In the precious moments before client presentations, one sees consulting teams moving around the periphery of waiting rooms, looking for the best place for cell reception so that they can make calls. "My colleagues go to the ether when we wait for our clients," says one advertising executive, "I think our presentations have suffered." We live and work with people whose commitment to our presence feels increasingly tenuous because they are tethered to more important others. [...]

[...] TETHERED: TO WHOM/TO WHAT?

Acknowledging our tethered state opens up the question of two whom or what we are connected. Traditional telephones tied us to friends, family, colleagues from school and work, and commercial or philanthropic solicitations. Things are no longer so simple. These days we respond to humans and to objects that represent them: answering machines, websites, and personal pages on social networking sites. Sometimes we engage with avatars that anonymously "stand in" for others, enabling us to express ourselves in intimate ways to strangers, in part because we and they are able to veil who we "really are." And sometimes we listen to disembodied voices – recorded announcements and messages – or interact with synthetic voice recognition protocols that simulate real people as they try to assist us with technical and administrative problems. We no longer demand that as a person we have another person as an interlocutor. [...]

[...] Relationship artifacts are the latest chapter in the trajectory of the tethered self. We move from technologies that tether us to people to those that are able to tether us to the websites and avatars that represent people. Relational artifacts represent programmers, but are given autonomy, primitive psychologies, are designed to stand on their own as creatures to be loved. They are potent objects-to-think-with for asking the questions, posed by all of the machines that tether us to new socialities: "What is an authentic relationship with a machine?" "What are machines doing to our relationships with people?" and ultimately, "What is a relationship?"

REFERENCES

Amy Bruckman, 1992. *"Identity Workshop: Emergent Social and Psychological Phenomena in Text-Based Virtual Reality."* Unpublished paper written in partial completion of a doctoral degree at the Media Lab, Massachusetts Institute of Technology. http://www-static.cc.gatech.edu/~asb/papers/old-papers.html. accessed May 27, 2006.

Sue Campbell Clark, 2000. Work/family border theory: A new theory of work/family balance. *Human Relations,* 53(6), 747-770.

Stephan Desrochers and Leisa D. Sargent, 2003. (February 28 – March 1, 2003). *Work-Family Boundary Ambiguity, Gender and Stress in Dual-Earner Couples.* Paper presented at the Conference "From 9-to-5 to 24/7: How Workplace Changes Impact Families, Work, and Communities" 2003 BPW/Brandeis University Conference, Orlando, Florida.

Michael Foucault, 1979. *Discipline and Punish: The Birth of the Prison* (New York: Vintage Books).

Diana B. Gant and Sara Kiesler, 2001. "Blurring the Boundaries: Cell Phones, Mobility and the Line between Work and Personal Life," in N.G.R.H. Barry Brown (ed.), *Wireless World: Social and Interactional Aspects of the Mobile Age* (pp. 121-131): Springer.

Thomas R. Herzog, Andrea M. Black, Kimberlee A. Fountaine, and Deborah J. Knotts, 1997. Reflection and Attentional Recovery as Distinctive Benefits of Restorative Environments. *Journal of Environmental Psychology,* 17, 165-170.

Carolyn A. Jones, 2006. See "Tethered," in Carolyn A. Jones, ed., *Sensorium: Embodied Experience, Technology, and Contemporary Art* (Cambridge: List Visual Art Center and MIT Press, 2006).

Stephen Kaplan, 1995. The Restorative Benefits of Nature: Toward an Integrative Framework. *Journal of Environmental Psychology,* 15, 169-182.

Melissa Mazmanian, 2005, "Some Thoughts on BlackBerries." Memo.

Paul H. Ornstein, ed., 1978. *The Search for the Self: Selected Writings of Heinz Kohut: 1950-1978,* Volume 2. (New York: International Universities Press, Inc.).

David Riesman (with Reuel Denney and Nathan Glazer), 1950. *The Lonely Crowd: A Study of the Changing American Character* (New Haven: Yale University Press).

Michelle Shumate and Janet Fulk, 2004. Boundaries and role conflict when work and family are colocated: A communication network and symbolic interaction approach. *Human Relations,* 57(1), 55-74.

Sherry Turkle, 1995. *Life on the Screen: Identity in the Age of the Internet* (New York: Simon and Schuster).

Turkle, 1999. "Toys to Change our Minds," in Sian Griffiths, ed., *Predictions* (Oxford: Oxford University Press).

Turkle, 2003a. "Sociable Technologies: Enhancing Human Performance when the Computer is Not a Tool but a Companion," in Mihail C. Roco and William Sims Bainbridge, eds., Converging Technologies for Improving Human Performance (The Netherlands: Kluwer Academic Publishers).

Turkle, 2003b. "Technology and Human Vulnerability," *Harvard Business Review*, September 2003.

Turkle, 2004a. "Relational Artifacts." Final Report on Proposal to the National Science Foundation SES-01115668.

Turkle, 2004b. "Spinning Technology," in Marita Sturken, Douglas Thomas, and Sandra Bal-Rokeach, eds., *Technological Visions* (Philadelphia: Temple University Press).

Turkle, 2004c. "Whither Psychoanalysis in Computer Culture," *Psychoanalytic Psychology: Journal of the Division of Psychoanalysis*, American Psychological Association, Winter 2004.

Turkle, 2005a. *The Second Self: Computers and the Human Spirit* (Cambridge, MA: MIT Press [1984]).

Turkle, 2005b. "Computer Games as Evocative Objects: From Projective Screens to Relational Artifacts," in Joost Raessens, and Jeffrey Goldstein, eds. *Handbook of Computer Games Studies*. (Cambridge, Mass.: MIT Press).

Turkle, 2005c. "Relational Artifacts/Children/Elders: The Complexities of CyberCompanions," Stresa, Italy, IEEE Workshop on Android Science, July 2005.

Turkle, 2006a. "First Encounters with Kismet and Cog: Children's Relationship with Humanoid Robots" (with Cynthia Breazeal, Olivia Dasté, and Brian Scassellati), in Paul Messaris and Lee Humphreys, eds. *Digital Media: Transfer in Human Communication* (New York: Peter Lang Publishing).

Turkle, 2006b. Tamagotchi Diary. *The London Review of Books*, April 20, 2006.

Turkle, 2006c. "Tethering," in Carolyn A. Jones, ed., *Sensorium: Embodied Experience, Technology, and Contemporary Art* (Cambridge: List Visual Art Center and MIT Press).

Victor Turner, 1969. *The Ritual Process: Structure and Anti-Structure* (Chicago: Aldine).

Joseph Weizenbaum, 1976. Computer Power and Human Reason: From Judgment to Calculation (San Francisco, W.H. Freeman).

Collaborate

Turkle illustrates how we are often tethered—physically and emotionally—to technologies like iPods, cell phones, laptops, and others. With your classmates, attempt a weeklong "media diet" in which you untether yourself from as many technologies as you can. After the week is over, check back in. Who lasted the longest? Who caved in first? What did you learn from your week-long media diet?

Invent

What relationships do you have with the technologies that surround you? How do they reflect or help you form parts of your identity? Choose a technology that you can carry around with you, like a cell phone, iPod, laptop computer, or digital watch, and examine the ways that this technological object reflects aspects of your personality. How does this artifact extend your sense of self? When choosing your object, did aspects of your personality influence your choice of whether or not to buy this particular object?

"I fell into the computer realm from the typewriter dimension, then plugged my computer into my telephone and got sucked into the net." That's how Howard Rheingold explains over three decades of online involvement that has impacted how the world understands the idea of "virtual communities." His experiences with the Whole Earth 'Lectronic Link (the WELL), one of the oldest virtual communities online, was recounted in Rheingold's 1993 book The Virtual Community. *In "Look Who's Talking," published on Wired.com in January 1999, Rheingold turns his eye to a community which he is not a part of, the Amish, to examine some of our misconceptions about technology use among the Amish community.*

LOOK WHO'S TALKING

By Howard Rheingold

The Amish are famous for shunning technology. But their secret love affair with the cell phone is causing an uproar.

Technology is my native tongue. I'm online six hours a day. I have a cell phone, voicemail, fax, laptop, and palmtop. I'm connected—and lately, I've been wondering where all this equipment is leading me. I've found myself asking a question that's both disquieting and intriguing: What kind of person am I becoming as a result of all this stuff?

Of course, I'm not the only one asking. And a while ago it occurred to me that, in addition to measuring my reactions against those of others in comparable circumstances, I might learn something entirely new by looking at a civilization of which I am not a member. The Amish communities of Pennsylvania, despite the retro image of horse-drawn buggies and straw hats, have long been engaged in a productive debate about the consequences of technology. So I turned to them for a glimpse of the future.

Amish settlements have become a cliché for refusing technology. Tens of thousands of people wear identical, plain, homemade clothing, cultivate their rich fields with horse-drawn machinery, and live in houses lacking that basic modern spirit called electricity. But the Amish do use such 20th-century consumer technologies as disposable diapers, in-line skates, and gas barbecue grills. Some might call this combination paradoxical, even contradictory. But it could also be called sophisticated, because the Amish have an elaborate system by which they evaluate the tools they use; their tentative, at times reluctant use of technology is more complex than a simple rejection or a whole-hearted embrace. What if modern Americans could possibly agree upon criteria for acceptance, as the Amish have? Might we find better ways to wield technological power, other than simply unleashing it and seeing what happens? What can we learn from a culture that habitually negotiates the rules for new tools?

Last summer, armed with these questions and in the company of an acquaintance with Amish contacts, I traveled around the countryside of Lancaster County, Pennsylvania. Everywhere, there were freshly planted fields, farmhouses with handsome, immaculate barns and outbuildings. At one farm we passed, a woman was sitting a hundred yards from her house on the edge of a kitchen garden. She wore the traditional garb of the conservative Old Order—a long, unadorned dress sheathed by an apron, her hair covered by a prayer bonnet. She was sitting in the middle of the garden, alone, the very image of technology-free simplicity. But she was holding her hand up to her ear. She appeared to be intent on something, strangely engaged.

"Whenever you see an Amish woman sitting in the field like that," my guide said, "she's probably talking on a cell phone."

"It's a controversy in the making," he continued. A rather large one, it turns out—yet part of the continuum of determining whether a particular technology belongs in Amish life. They've adopted horses, kerosene lamps, and propane refrigerators; should they add cell phones?

Collective negotiations over the use of telephones have ignited intense controversies in the Amish community since the beginning of the 20th century. In fact, a dispute over the role of the phone was the principal issue behind the 1920s division of the Amish church, wherein one-fifth of the membership broke away to form their own church.

Eventually, certain Amish communities accepted the telephone for its aid in summoning doctors and veterinarians, and in calling suppliers. But even these Amish did not allow the telephone into the home. Rather, they required that phones be used communally. Typically, a neighborhood of two or three extended families shares a telephone housed in a wooden shanty, located either at the intersection of several fields or at the end of a common lane.

These structures look like small bus shelters or privies; indeed, some phones are in outhouses. Sometimes the telephone shanties have answering machines in them. (After all, who wants to wait in the privy on the off chance someone will call?)

The first Amish person I contacted, I reached by answering machine. He was a woodworker who, unlike some of his brethren, occasionally talked to outsiders. I left a message on his phone, which I later learned was located in a shanty in his neighbor's pasture. The next day the man, whom I'll call Amos, returned my call. We agreed to meet at his farmstead a few days later.

I couldn't help thinking it was awfully complicated to have a phone you used only for calling back—from a booth in a meadow. Why not make life easier and just put one in the house?

"What would that lead to?" another Amish man asked me. "We don't want to be the kind of people who will interrupt a conversation at home to answer a telephone. It's not just how you use the technology that concerns us. We're also concerned about what kind of person you become when you use it."

> Far from knee-jerk technophobes, these are very adaptive techno-selectives who devise remarkable technologies that fit within their self-imposed limits.

The Amish are famously shy. Their commitment to "plain" living is most obvious in their unadorned clothing—Old Order Amish even eschew buttons, requiring humble hooks instead. Any sign of individuality is cause for concern. Until fairly recently, Amish teachers would reprimand the student who raised his or her hand as being too individualistic. Calling attention to oneself, or being "prideful," is one of the cardinal Amish worries. Having your name or photo in the papers, even talking to the press, is almost a sin.

Like most modern Americans, I assume individuality is not only a fundamental value, but a goal in life, an art form. The garish technicolor shirts and hand-painted shoes I usually wear sometimes startle business audiences who show up for my speaking engagements. My reasoning: If I think for myself, why not dress for myself? Dye technology has given us all these colors, so let's use 'em! Still, I didn't want to make my idiosyncrasies the focus of my visit to Amish country. So I bought a plain blue work shirt, dark blue gabardine pants, and brown shoes. I hadn't traveled so drably in many years.

Amos runs a factory of sorts in the vicinity of three memorably named Pennsylvania towns: Bird-in-Hand, Paradise, and Intercourse. The sun was setting as I drove slowly down his unpaved driveway. I found myself inside a tableau that must have looked almost exactly the same 200 years ago. Several men and young boys in identical black trousers, suspenders, and straw hats were operating horse-drawn equipment in the fields beyond. One of Amos's grandsons pointed me to a plain wooden building beside the barn.

The aroma of cows gave way to the pungent smell of diesel fuel and wood chips as I entered the workshop. The whine of a wood-milling machine made it futile to talk. This was not the serene place the words "Amish woodshop" conjure up. My host finished cutting a 12-foot-long plank before we greeted each other. He then lit a kerosene lamp in the small office next to his workshop and invited me in. The office had no modern technology in it, but railroad posters were tacked on the walls, and wooden locomotive models sat on the shelves.

Amos had sawdust and hydraulic fluid in his beard. His blue-gray eyes fastened on me as he bounced back his own questions in reply to my queries. He had received the same eighth-grade education that all Amish youth are given, but it was obvious that Amos did some outside reading. When I asked him to describe his sense of community, he started out, "Hmm, how do you pronounce s-c-e-n-a-r-i-o?"

Amos runs a successful business crafting wooden furniture, which he sells throughout Pennsylvania and beyond—primarily to the "English" (the Amish term for non-Amish). It's a trade more and more Amish are getting into. Inside Amos's home there are no telephones, radios, televisions, vacuum cleaners, dishwashers, or other electrical appliances. In his shop, routers, mills, and sanders are powered by specially adapted hydraulic mechanisms connected to a diesel engine located near a large open door, exhausting outside the building.

This was a good case study in Amish reasoning: Far from knee-jerk technophobes, these are very adaptive techno-selectives who devise remarkable technologies that fit within their self-imposed limits. The price of good farmland and the number of Amish families are both increasing so rapidly that in recent decades they have adopted nonagricultural enterprises for livelihood—woodworking, construction, light factory work. This, in turn, has forced the Amish to adopt technologies that can enhance their productivity. And the interface with the English brings its own set of demands: When the State of Pennsylvania refused to certify Amish-produced milk unless it was stirred mechanically and refrigerated according to state health codes, the Amish installed stirring machines and refrigeration—operated by batteries or propane gas.

Amos, like many other Amish craftsmen, uses electricity in his workshop for certain tools. But the electricity does not come from public utility lines. Amos runs a diesel generator to charge a bank of 12-volt batteries. The batteries' DC charge is then sent through a converter to create homegrown 110-volt "Amish electricity." To generate more, he has to haul the diesel fuel in from town on his horse-drawn buggy.

> "Does it bring us together, or draw us apart?" is the question bishops ask in considering whether to permit or put away a technology.

To the obvious question why allow Amish electricity but not public electricity, Amos answered slowly and deliberately, "The Bible teaches us not to conform to the world, to keep a separation. Connecting to the electric lines would make too many things too easy. Pretty soon, people would start plugging in radios and televisions, and that's like a hot line to the modern world. We use batteries and generators because you can use the batteries for only a short time and because you have to fuel and maintain the generator yourself. It's a way of controlling our use of electricity. We try to restrict things that would lead to us losing that sense of being separate, to put the brakes on how fast we change."

Despite the reputation today's Amish have as old-fashioned diehards, their departure from Europe several centuries ago was driven by their success as innovators. They started out as radical religious libertarians—at a time when the price of religious radicalism was martyrdom. Catholics and Protestants were killing each other in a major religious war, but both sides took a serious dislike to these defiant theological purists, known at the time as Anabaptists, for their emphasis on adult baptism. (Today, every Amish household has a copy of *Martyrs' Mirror*, a text of more than 1,000 pages that details the excruciating and humiliating public executions suffered by Anabaptist martyrs in Switzerland, Germany, and Holland.) The Anabaptists developed a soil technology based on crop rotation, planting clover in their pastures, and sweetening their earth with lime and gypsum; they dramatically increased the yield of their land, and some of them became wealthy.

Ironically, those same Anabaptists helped set the stage for the fast-paced changes of modern life that today's Amish reject. It was the widespread adoption of Anabaptist practices that eventually produced enough food to free other agricultural laborers, creating the workforce that would be needed for the industrial revolution.

Toward the end of the 17th century, one of the Anabaptist leaders, Jakob Ammann, decided that his Swiss brethren had not been radical enough. Ammann and his followers, who came to be known as "Amish," broke with traditional Anabaptists, moved to the New World, and started farming in Lancaster County in 1710.

In today's Pennsylvania Amish country, a group of 20 to 30 families who live near one another constitute a "district." Each district has a bishop, and the bishops get together twice a year to discuss church matters. This includes raising the recurring questions about which technologies should be permitted in the community, and which banned or regulated.

While the say of the bishops is binding, the Amish come to their decisions quite consensually. New things are not outright forbidden, nor is there a rush to judgment. Rather, technologies filter in when one of the more daring members of the community starts to use, or even purchases, something new. Then others try it. Then reports circulate about the results. What happens with daily use? Does it bring people together? Or have the opposite effect?

Despite the almost organic ebb and flow of this evaluation process, the common goal is constant submission to the judgment of one's peers. On my visit, I was constantly struck by what seemed an alien conception of community. As a kid I was encouraged to "do my thing" while being nice to others; I've lived in five states and dozens of neighborhoods. Amish communities are not just tightly knit and immobile, they're authoritarian.

Yet there is some room for disagreement; consider how the bishops judged the automobile in the 1960s. Typically, the Amish have large extended families; most have dozens of cousins within walking or buggy distance. Every other Sunday, instead of attending church, the Amish are encouraged to visit relatives and the sick. Over time, it was felt that the automobile was enlarging people's traveling radius too far beyond their extended family, to diversions and recreations not related to the community, decreasing the social cohesion and personal connection the Amish so cherish. Some bishops accepted the use of the automobile under certain conditions, while others rejected it outright. The Amish are now split into traditional "Old Order" Amish who still stick to horse and buggy, "New Order" Amish who approve use of telephones and powered farm equipment but shun public electricity, and "Beachy Amish," named for the '20s liberal leader Moses Beachy, who permit both public electricity and automobiles.

While all orders now allow diesel engines in the barn to blow silage, their use is still resisted in the fields—the bishops don't want increased efficiency to interfere with the practice of fathers and sons, mothers and daughters, working together with horse-drawn machinery and handheld implements. Notably, some Old Order Amish allow some diesel-powered equipment in the fields—if it's hauled by animals. "Does it bring us together, or draw us apart?" is the primary question the bishops ask in considering whether to permit or put away a technology.

The bishops' rulings can take decades. In daily life, the Amish take their directions in dress, thought, behavior, and custom from a body of unwritten but detailed rules known as the "Ordnung." Individuals and communities maintain a separation from the world (by not connecting their houses to telephones or electricity), a closeness to one another (through regular meetings), and an attitude of humility so specific they have a name for it ("Gelassenheit"). Decisions about technology hinge on these collective criteria. If a telephone in the home interferes with face-to-face visiting, or an electrical hookup fosters unthinking dependence on the outside world, or a new pickup truck in the driveway elevates one person above his neighbors, then people start to talk about it. The talk reaches the bishops' ears.

In the middle of Amish country, it occurs to me that Internet culture itself grew out of a kind of virtual Ordnung—the norms of cooperation, information-sharing, and netiquette taught to newbies by the first

> Instead of a telephone shanty, some Old Order Amish leave their cell phone overnight with an English neighbor, who recharges it.

generations of users. The celebrated "anarchy" of the early days was possible only because of the near-universal adherence to largely unwritten rules. But the Internet population has grown fast—so fast that the sudden influx of tens of millions of newbies has overwhelmed the capacity of the old-timers to pass on the Ordnung. In the process, the Internet loses its unique hallmarks, coming to resemble and reflect the rest of contemporary culture.

"The Amish employ an intuitive sense about what will build solidarity and what will pull them apart," says Donald Kraybill, author of *The Riddle of Amish Culture*. "You find state-of-the-art barbecues on some Amish porches. Here is a tool they see as increasing family coherence: Barbecues bring people together." Asked what kinds of questions the bishops will likely raise about cell phones, Kraybill replies, "Are cell phones being used 'to make a living' or just for gossip and frivolous chatter? Will permitting cell phones lead to having phones in homes, and where will that lead ... to fax machines and the Internet?"

"We don't want to stop progress, we just want to slow it down," several Amish told me. Conversations about technology often turn on where to "hold the line" against the too-rapid advance of innovation. Riding in automobiles to work, but not owning them, putting telephone shanties in fields, requiring battery power instead of electrical lines are all ways of holding the line.

And clearly a lot could be learned about the Amish hold-the-line philosophy by looking at those who either crossed the line or pushed it further out. So I sought out several of the more boldly experimental members of the greater Plain community (Amish and Mennonites and other religious groups sharing a kindred commitment to plain living). In ranging from farmers who ran small enterprises in barnside sheds to well-equipped machine workshops and multimillion-dollar crafts factories, I soon was directed to Moses Smucker, who runs a harness shop in Churchtown, Pennsylvania.

Moses is an early adopter. He didn't mind if I used his real name, a liberty that has made him the subject of a few other journalists' stories. When I arrived at his manufacturing headquarters, I took a look at some of the harnesses on display—one of them had a price tag of $12,000. If you've ever seen the Budweiser Clydesdales Christmas commercials, you've seen harness bells from Moses Smucker's Churchtown workshop.

In the back of the store, more than a dozen young Amish men were working at modern machinery powered by hydraulics and diesel-generated electricity. Upstairs, I saw a woman in traditional plain clothing seated in front of a PC.

Moses Smucker might look like Abe Lincoln, in his black suit and mustache-free beard, but he bore the same time-is-money air of any factory manager taking a few minutes out of a busy day to talk to the press. Where Amos was rough hewn and wry, Moses seemed shrewd and slick. His office was certainly in a different century from Amos's. An electronic rolodex and an electric calculator sat atop an old roll-top desk. I noticed a clock in the shape of a horse and buggy. The whip ticked back and forth.

"When I started this business in 1970," Moses said, "it wasn't accepted to have a telephone in the building, even in a business. But the telephone began to be accepted through popular disobedience. More businesses put them in and the bishops didn't stop them."

Will the bishops also eventually allow phones in the home? I asked.

"When the telephone first came out here, people put them in their homes," explained Moses. "But they were party lines. One time a woman overheard two other women gossiping about her. She objected. That wasn't what we wanted for our families or our community, so the bishops met and home telephones were banned."

> Is the family meal enhanced by a beeper? Who exactly benefits from call waiting? Is automated voicemail a hint about how institutions value human life?

I had heard the same story from several other Amish—in fact, this story seemed to be a key part of community mythology. A writer named Diane Zimmerman Umble, who grew up in Lancaster County and had family roots in the Plain orders, traced the story to its origin, a 1986 memoir written by an Old Order Amishman born in 1897. As a graduate student, Zimmerman Umble started investigating Amish community telephones for a course on contemporary social theory, and ended up writing a book on the subject, *Holding the Line: The Telephone in Old Order Mennonite and Amish Life.* Among her findings was the power of anecdote in the Amish decisionmaking process.

Anecdote, of course, is a key currency on the Internet, so I asked Moses if he'd heard stories about it. Although he used a computer in his business, he didn't believe the Internet as currently constituted would ever be permitted. Based on anecdotal evidence, he said, "It's too unregulated, there's too much trash, and there's a worry people will use it for purposes unrelated to work."

I asked another Amish workshop owner whom I'll call Caleb what he thought about technology. He pulled some papers out of a file cabinet, handed them to me, and said, "I share some of this fellow's opinions," pointing to a magazine interview with virtual reality pioneer Jaron Lanier. Asked for an opinion he shared with the dreadlocked-and- dashikied Jaron, he replied, "I agree with his statement that you can't design foolproof machines, because fools are so clever."

Caleb also discussed the Amish resistance to becoming "modern." They're not worried about becoming people without religion or people who use lots of technology, he explained; rather, the Amish fear assimilating the far more dangerous ideas that "progress" and new technologies are usually beneficial, that individuality is a precious value, that the goal of life is to "get ahead." This mind-set, not specific technologies, is what the Amish most object to.

"The thing I noticed about the telephone is the way it invades who you are," Caleb said. "We're all losing who we are because of the telephone and other machines—not just the Amish."

In *Holding the Line,* Zimmerman Umble writes: "Some Old Order people feel that relaxation of telephone rules reflects a movement toward an 'uncontrollable drift' which must be halted. Others see these steps as pragmatic choices necessary to hold the community together economically. The paradox in the Old Order story is that the telephone does both: It holds people together by making communication among community members possible, and it separates them from the world and from each other. The telephone is both evil and good."

Donald Kraybill, who is also provost of Messiah College, on the outskirts of Amish country, believes taboos about telephones are "a symbolic way of keeping the technology at a distance and making it your servant, rather than the other way around."

Can they make the cell phone a servant? My questions on this score were answered mostly with anecdote. I heard of one Amish man who was going to be late to a chiropractor appointment, so he pulled out his cell phone and called the receptionist from the bus he was on. Zimmerman Umble heard of a Plain order businessman who called his stockbroker from his company car phone, pushing three taboos at once past their boundaries.

Zimmerman Umble pointed out that part of what makes cell phones so handy— the lack of a wire—also poses a special challenge for the Amish. "In the early part of the community discussion, electrical and telephone lines carried substantial symbolic freight," she said. The wires meant that anyone in the community could easily see who was using electricity and phones. "But now, in the absence of the line, behavior can't be monitored in the same way. It is harder to maintain separation between home and business when you have a cell phone in your pocket. In that sense it tests the community consensus about what is allowable."

Calling around cell phone outlets in the Lancaster area, I found a merchant who has been selling cell phones to Plain folk for years. "A great percentage of my customer base is Amish and Mennonite," the merchant told me. "More Amish than Mennonite. We opened our cellular system 12 years ago. Within the first year, I had an Amish customer. He first called from his neighbor's house. He owned a painting business and told me he wasn't allowed to have a cell phone personally, but his bishop said he could buy one for his foreman to use in the company truck. It didn't take too long before I started getting quite a lot of telephone calls from the Amish."

This raised quite a few interesting consumer technology questions. Ordinarily, for example, one needs a credit card (and good credit) to secure a cell phone. "The Amish pay in cash," explained the merchant, who, along with most Amish-friendly shopkeepers, didn't want his name used. "We normally ask for a driver's license for the purpose of identification when we activate cellular service—of course, the Amish don't have driver's licenses. They weren't able to get phones for several months, since we weren't allowed to open accounts without driver's licenses. So we had to make a policy change to accommodate them. We ended up asking for another form of identification. But the Amish don't believe in photography, so we couldn't get a photo ID. Eventually we told them to get Pennsylvania state IDs without photographs.

"I've sold hundreds of cell phones to them, primarily business phones," the merchant continued, adding a few details about how the phones were used. "Some Old Order Amish leave their cell phones in their shanty. Some leave the phone overnight with an English neighbor, who recharges it for them; then the Amish pick up the phone in the morning."

It's a pretty safe prediction that when the bishops get around to their formal ruling, cell phones will not be deemed appropriate for personal use. In the 1910s, when the telephone was only beginning to change the world at large, the Old Order Amish recognized that the caller at the other end of the line was an interloper, someone who presumed to take precedence over the family's normal, sacred, communications. Keeping the telephone in an unheated shanty in a field, or even an outhouse, was keeping the phone in its proper place.

Though the Amish determination to allow phones at work but ban them at home might seem hard to accept, I appreciate the deliberation put into their decision. In fact, similar reflection might highlight conflicts between our own practices and values. How often do we interrupt a conversation with someone who is physically present in order to answer the telephone? Is the family meal enhanced by a beeper? Who exactly is benefiting from call waiting? Is automated voicemail a dark hint about the way our institutions value human time and life? Can pagers and cell phones that vibrate instead of ring solve the problem? Does the enjoyment of virtual communities by growing numbers of people enhance or erode citizen participation in the civic life of geographic communities?

"What does the Old Order story have to say to members of postmodern society?" asks Diane Zimmerman Umble. "The struggle of Old Order groups to mold technology in the service of community provides a provocative model of resistance for those who have come to recognize that technology brings both benefits and costs.... Their example invites reflection on a modern dilemma: how to balance the rights of the individual with the needs of the community. For them, community comes first."

Indeed, what does one's use of a tool say to other people, particularly loved ones, about where they stand in our priorities? In my own house, we decided to get a rollover to voicemail instead of call waiting—experiences on the receiving end of call waiting convinced us that both parties on the other end of the line get pissed off when you interrupt the conversation. No matter how absorbing the flame war of the moment might be, I make a point of suspending online communication when someone in my presence attempts to talk with me. And I've come to believe that face-to-face conversation should outrank disembodied conversation via cell phone or email.

I never expected the Amish to provide precise philosophical yardsticks that could guide the use of technological power. What drew me in was their long conversation with their tools. We technology-enmeshed "English" don't have much of this sort of discussion. And yet we'll need many such conversations, because a modern heterogeneous society is going to have different values, different trade-offs, and different discourses. It's time we start talking about the most important influence on our lives today.

I came away from my journey with a question to contribute to these conversations: If we decided that community came first, how would we use our tools differently?

Rheingold describes the complicated relationship that the Amish have with technology by noting that they are "very adaptive techno-selectives who devise remarkable technologies that fit within their self-imposed limits." Write a reflective essay that explores your techno-selectivity: What kinds of limits do you have? What technologies will you not use and why? What online activities will you not participate in and why? How have you adapted to a world surrounded by technology in a way that helps you fit within your limits comfortably?

According to Rheingold, the primary question that Amish leaders ask when considering the inclusion of new technologies in the Amish communities is "Does it bring us together, or draw us apart?" Choose a technology—a cell phone; a social networking site; e-mail; Twitter; word processing; and so on. List ways that you see this technology being able to bring a group of people together and how the technology might also push people apart.

Rheingold notes that "the Amish have an elaborate system by which they evaluate the tools they use; their tentative, at times reluctant use of technology is more complex than a simple rejection or a whole-hearted embrace. What if modern Americans could possibly agree upon criteria for acceptance, as the Amish have? Might we find better ways to wield technological power, other than simply unleashing it and seeing what happens?" With a group of your classmates, collaborate to come up with a set of criteria that we might use before bringing a new technology into our lives (or perhaps before upgrading to the latest and greatest version of a technology already owned). What kinds of criteria for accepting a new technology do you believe we might create so that we are satisfied by the technologies we eventually include in our lives?

(E)DENTITY

In 2008, Nicholas Carr asked the provocative question "Is Google Making Us Stupid?" in The Atlantic; *the book* The Shallows: What the Internet is Doing to Our Brains *followed in 2010. In these pieces, Carr critiques the effect of constant online searching and reading on our abilities to pay attention and sustain ideas for long periods of time. In "The Love Song of J. Alfred Prufrock's Avatar," published online in 2006 on Carr's blog "Rough Type," the author uses a poem by T. S. Eliot as a framework to discuss online identity through the construction of avatars. In the pages after his blog post, you will see avatars and their real-life counterparts from Tracy Spaight, Robbie Cooper, and Julian Dibbell's 2009 book* Alter Ego: Avatars and Their Creators.

THE LOVE SONG OF J. ALFRED PRUFROCK'S AVATAR

By Nicholas Carr

> *There will be time, there will be time*
> *To prepare a face to meet the faces that you meet …*
>
> —T.S. Eliot

Yes, now I see it, the next great affliction to bedevil the self-consuming American psyche: avatar anxiety.

In the current issue of the New Yorker, John Cassidy writes about the business and sociology of community web sites, looking in particular at the origins and development of the vast student site Facebook. He describes how the moves Facebook is making to expand and become profitable may undermine what made it popular in the first place. By inviting in high school students, for instance, it has—surprise!—alienated some of its original college-student members. And by allowing members to upload photographs of other students, it has muddied the privacy protections that many members cherish. In short, as it pursues and emulates industry-leader MySpace, Facebook is becoming a less intimate, less exclusive, less protected place.

Monetization changes everything.

But that's not what I found most interesting about Cassidy's piece. Rather, it was his discussion of the motivations of the people who join social networks and create online identities. What does our eagerness to construct symbolic selves—what the knowing call "avatars"—say about us and where we're headed?

Cassidy quotes the sociologist Duncan Watts on the broad appeal of community sites: "Now everyone is used to the idea that we are connected [through the internet], and that's not so interesting. If I had to guess why sites like Facebook are so popular, I would say it doesn't have anything to do with networking at all. It's voyeurism and exhibitionism." Cassidy sees other forces at work as well, suggesting that "the success of sites like MySpace and Facebook may have less to do with the opportunities they provide for self-expression than with peer pressure" and the sites' "power to confer social standing." He quotes a Facebook member: "I tried to hold out and go against the flow. But so many of my friends were members that I finally gave in." Adds Facebook cofounder Chris Hughes: "If you don't have a Facebook profile, you don't have an online identity ... You don't exist—online, at least. That's why we get so many people to join up. You need to be on it."

In what may be the most revealing passage in the article, a member named Matt, a recent Yale graduate, describes the Prufrockian anxiety he feels in constructing his online identity. "I want to seem self-aware," he says, "but not a pretentious asshole." He goes on to explain why he chose to portray himself with a photograph that shows him "with his eyes closed and his mouth stuffed with cookies":

> "I think it's something of an achievement to fit six Oreos in one's mouth, and, more to the point, it relieves me of having to put up a picture with which I'm actually trying to convince people that I look good. In short, I wouldn't put anything up that I wouldn't want everyone to see, and I want certain people to get much more out of it than others, and for those certain to be impressed by my cleverness tempered by restraint."

Do I dare to eat a peach?

To hear that people are vain, even obsessively so, is not surprising. Still, though, there's something sad about this—funny-sad, anyway. Your online self, like Matt's, is entirely self-created, and because it determines your identity and social standing in an internet community, each decision you make about how you portray yourself—about which facts (or falsehoods) to reveal, which photos to upload, which people "to friend," which bands or movies or books to list as favorites, which words to put in a blog—is fraught, subtly or not, with a kind of existential danger. And you are entirely responsible for the consequences as you navigate that danger. You are, after all, your avatar's parents; there's no one else to blame. So leaving the real world to participate in an online community—or a virtual world like Second Life—doesn't relieve the anxiety of self-consciousness; it magnifies it. You become more, not less, exposed. To again quote Eliot's Prufrock, it is:

> *as if a magic lantern threw the nerves in patterns on a screen.*

If I were of a mind to launch a Web 2.0 business today, I wouldn't rely on advertising or subscriptions or try to maximize my page views. I wouldn't worry about technology at all, in fact. I'd become a personal avatar consultant, helping nervous people construct and manage their menagerie of online selves. Or else I'd become a psychotherapist specializing in "avatar issues," maybe even renting an office in Second Life with a little virtual couch. I'd tell Matt, for instance, that perhaps that Oreo picture wasn't the best way to fulfill his Facebook aspirations. I would, in short, find a way to capitalize on what promises to be a lucrative epidemic of avatar anxiety.

What makes me confident of the success of such an endeavor is a recently announced Facebook feature that, as Cassidy describes it, "allows users to create a second profile that omits some of the content of their original one." Here's how the site is promoting the new feature: "Would you prefer that your vegan friends don't see that photo of you eating a giant steak? You can establish a Limited Profile that will create a limited view of your Facebook profile for selected people. These people will not be informed that they are not able to see certain profile features." You see where this is going, of course. You'll have not only your Facebook self and your MySpace self and your Second Life self and maybe your TagWorld self and your Doppelganger self, but within each of these communities you'll be able to formulate various alternative selves tailored to different audiences. And you'll have to suffer the social consequences of every decision involved in every act of self-formulation.

So many faces to prepare. So many decisions and revisions. Oh, J. Alfred, you died too soon.

And when I am formulated, sprawling on a pin,

When I am pinned and wriggling on the wall,

Then how should I begin

To spit out all the butt-ends of my days and ways?

And how should I presume?

ALTER EGO AVATARS

Photograph by Robbie Cooper

NAME Jason Rowe
BORN 1974
OCCUPATION None
LOCATION Crosby, Tex.
AVATAR NAME Rurouni Kenshin
AVATAR CREATED 2003
GAME PLAYED Star Wars Galaxies
HOURS PER WEEK IN-GAME 80
CHARACTER TYPE Human marksman, rifleman
SPECIAL ABILITIES Ranged weapon specialization

Photograph by Robbie Cooper

NAME Kimberly Rufer-Bach
BORN 1966
OCCUPATION Software developer
LOCATION Clarksville, Tenn.
AVATAR NAME Kim Anubis
AVATAR CREATED 2004
GAME PLAYED Second Life
HOURS PER WEEK IN-GAME 70
CHARACTER TYPE Content creator
SPECIAL ABILITIES Building interactive objects

Photograph by Robbie Cooper

NAME Rebecca Glasure
BORN 1979
OCCUPATION Housewife
LOCATION Redding, Calif.
AVATAR NAME Stygian Physic
AVATAR CREATED 2005
GAME PLAYED City of Heroes
HOURS PER WEEK IN-GAME 25 to 30
CHARACTER TYPE Human mutant
SPECIAL ABILITIES Healing and dark-energy manipulation

After reading "The Love Song of J. Alfred Prufrock's Avatar" and exploring the avatars from *Alter Ego*, choose a site where you can create or choose an avatar to represent yourself. For example, you might create an avatar for a video or computer game, Second Life, or a site like Meez.com. Then, write an essay in which you explore some of the choices you made as you constructed your avatar. Describe the decisions you made when choosing or adapting its gender, its race, its physical characteristics and so on. Does your avatar reflect how you look and act in the real world or is it a reflection of something else? Were there aspects of your personality that you were not able to showcase through your avatar? Were there things you wished you could change about your avatar that the software or site would not let you do? If so, what? How did these constraints affect the ways that you were able to represent yourself online?

Carr describes a world where we each may have "various alternative selves tailored to different audiences." In your experience, do you find that your friends, relatives, and acquaintances online have alternative selves for different audiences in the sites you participate in? How about yourself? Are your profiles, avatars, and pictures on different sites generally similar or wildly different? Why or why not?

T. L. Taylor's 2006 book Play Between Worlds: Exploring Online Game Culture *shatters myths that online video games are only played by teenage boys disconnected from the real world. The chapter from her book excerpted here, "Where the Women Are," dismisses stereotypes about female gamers and the characters they choose when playing. Although women make up a substantial portion of online game play, they are often not directly marketed toward or targeted by game developers. In this selection from* Play Between Worlds, *Taylor explores how game play, character offerings, marketing, and combat battles all work as gendered spaces.*

excerpt from

WHERE THE WOMEN ARE

BY T.L. TAYLOR

Think for a moment about "gamers." Who do you imagine? If you create an image in your mind, what do they look like? Who are they? What is their life like? So far this book has proposed some counters to the common stereotypes.

I hope that the notion of gamer as social isolate has been eroded somewhat. But what about the gender of the imagined player? Typically the picture of gamers remains that of boys and men. Powerfully, this is often even the case for the women who themselves play games and who, when asked, still hesitate to call themselves gamers.[1] Women and girls who play computer games are, if not invisible, typically seen as oddballs and anomalies. But is it time to alter that internal model we often have? What can games like *EverQuest tell* us about the present, and future, of women and computer games?

A 2001 study by the market-research firm PC Data Online received a fair amount of press as it, for the first time ever, placed women as surpassing men in the population of online gamers (Guernsey 2001). While the margin was quite slim (50.4%), similar studies since then suggest a more diverse community of game players than previously thought. Aleks Krotoski, in a 2005 white paper commissioned by the Entertainment and Leisure Software Publishers

Association (ELSPA), has found that women make up 39% of all active gamers in the United States, while in Korea they go well beyond 50% of the market. She additionally suggests that they make up a sizable portion of the market for online browser-based gaming. While statistically gauging where female players fit in still requires more work, the image long held that women are not interested in or are not actually playing computer games (a potentially powerful distinction) must be reevaluated. This is not a trivial methodological point. As Simeon J. Yates and Karen Littleton suggest, "By focusing on their absence from gaming culture such research ignores the voices of those women and girls who do engage with computer games" (1999, 567).

While many of the women playing online are involved with more traditional sorts of games such as *Hearts* or *Bingo* (often played through major portals like Yahoo! Games),[2] a growing number play MMOGs. Though the number of women do not outpace men, officials at three major MMOGs *(Asheron's Call, Ultima Online*, and *EverQuest)* counted women as 20-30% of their subscriber base (Laber 2001). For more "casual" MMOGs, like *Yohoho! Puzzle Pirates* by Three Rings, women make up 40% of their player base.[3] Indeed, *EverQuest's* Gordon Wrinn has suggested that "the gateway for getting women into gaming is going to be through these role-playing games" (Laber 2001, 2).

This genre, then, offers a chance to revisit the question of women and gaming. While much of the literature so far has focused on the look of *Tomb Raider's* Lara Croft or the need for more "girl games," MMOGs push us to think about the pleasures those 20-30% of players are experiencing. Often the women and girls playing what are typically defined as masculine games are considered simply exceptions, data points that are outliers to be written off. But taking this demographic as a central focus of research is key to understanding the complexities around gender and computer games. Why is it women enjoy this kind of game, despite the fact that it has not been explicitly designed with them in mind, and in fact at times actively disenfranchises them?

SOCIAL AND IDENTITY PLAY

Women's general use of technology and the Internet often is framed around how they enjoy communicating with others and how engaged they are with experimenting with identity. Similarly, this is the major focus when women and gaming are discussed. As Patricia Pizer, a lead designer at Turbine (makers of the MMOG *Asheron's Call)* notes, "what women are finding so interesting about these games is that they provide a sense of community and social structure you don't see in other games" (Laber 2001,1). Chatting, connecting with other people, forming relationships and maintaining them are all aspects of the interpersonal pleasure MMOGs afford, and multiuser games have benefited by drawing in this component of online life. It is certainly the case that the women I spoke with over the years enjoy this aspect of the game.

However, it is important to recognize the multilayered nature of social life in such spaces. The most basic understanding of online socialization frames the activity in terms of "chat"—that you simply talk to people in the digital environment. However, much as offline, there are variations to social life and community that are quite rich, so we should be cautious about using shorthand explanations of the depth of work that goes into the social life of a space. Approaches that frame women as "wanting to talk" underplay the ways in which they are social actors whose interactions and identities are diverse and context specific. People move through a variety of spaces, all having their own set of norms and goals that have to be negotiated. We have seen, for example, the ways MMOGs put the user in many settings: within a guild, among intimates, among acquaintances, among strangers, with enemies and opposing guilds, with teams, within message boards, and within particular servers. Each of these settings bring with it an attendant group of specificities that must be accounted for when trying to understand not only how people game, but why they game in particular ways at particular times. Talking about how women simply like the "social" component of games, or how they like to "chat" can flatten a fairly rich play landscape and trivialize the work involved in sustaining social life within a game.

"Identity exploration" is also typically seen as a primary play goal for women and girls. Both because of the nature of the game (in which a character is created) and the engagement with avatars, users can construct identities that may or may not correlate to their offline persona. Much as with work on MUDs, we find examples of people experimenting with creating selves. Sherry Turkle, noted MIT researcher specializing on identity in a digital age, has argued: "When we step through the screen into virtual communities, we reconstruct our identities on the other side of the looking glass" (Turkle 1995, 178). Users are not formally bound to play only characters that correspond to their offline gender or to create identities that simply mirror their "real world" temperaments. Indeed, there is a long tradition within RPG culture to try and inhabit characters that are quite opposite of how a player might normally think and act outside of the game.

While we must consider critically how much freedom people have in reconstructing themselves online, virtual environments without a doubt remain a space in which users are constantly creating and performing a variety of identities.[4]

Given that *EverQuest* allows people to create up to eight distinct characters per server, there is at least formally a potential to explore a range of personae. It is not uncommon to find longtime players with several active or semi-active characters per account, though generally confined to one server.

When users do branch out onto other servers, it is often to play within particular rule sets, such as those that support strict role playing or PvP activity.[5] One notable phenomenon is the way information about characters is shared with friends and guild-mates, thereby plugging into preexisting community structures. Rather than keeping identities secret from one another, it is not uncommon for players to know who their friends' alternate characters are. There are exceptions to this of course (sometimes people only share such information with a select group) but overall the terrain of identity play in £Q is something more akin to parallel or linked character threads than firm persona boundaries.

The power of the avatar, however, does not have to come strictly through role playing, but also in the ways it serves as the key artifact through which users not only know others and the world around them, but themselves. Avatars are objects that not only represent people in the virtual world, but influence and propel the formation of identity and relationships. Jackie described the connection that developed:

[I] spent so much time expressing myself as her and interacting with people as her. And that's one of those things of course, as you develop your relationships with people as your online avatar you understand that they generally relate to you as your online avatar and not as you the person. I mean they know you aren't really an Elf and they probably, like, don't socially regard you as an Elf or anything like that but nonetheless they refer to you by your avatar's name, they base their experience and perception of you entirely on events that have occurred in the game involving your avatar. There are all these people I know who exist for me only in terms of my interactions with their avatar. I don't know really how old they are, what they do. It's all based on the avatar thing.

From the initial moment of character creation through the life of the player in the game, they fashion for themselves unique identities in the world. As they progress they are able to further customize themselves by choosing a surname and obtaining different objects. In a world in which you might very well run into two Barbarian Warriors with the exact same face, distinguishing oneself through naming and outfitting becomes key. While there is a significant focus on choosing particular clothing and weapons for very utilitarian reasons (better statistics being predominant), many women I have spoken to discuss enjoying how they have been able to customize their character in particular ways.

In nongame virtual worlds users often find the lines between their offline and online self fairly blurry (Taylor 2002; Turkle 1995). My sense is that while this happens much less in EQ, in large part because of its "gameness" always foregrounding its own intentionality—it is never *just* about identity play—avatars continue to present themselves as evocative vehicles for identity and MMOGs offer some unique possibilities. The issue of how virtual-world experiences "filter back" is particularly striking, though, when women report that playing the game helped them become more confident or assertive. One female player recounted encouraging the younger women she encountered in the game to use conflicts as an opportunity to practice more assertive behavior. Speaking about a guild-mate in particular, she said: "So I've been telling her, build a little backbone, don't be afraid to tell people what you think. It might hurt their feelings, it might make you an enemy, but what can they do?" Given the kind of identification with characters some users experience, this can be a powerful component of the game. As Katinka put it: "There's a little bit of yourself in your character, for my characters anyway. With my druid [I'm a] raw nature, nature-loving, tree-hugging girl. [And] I love animals, I love nature, so part of me is in her." While gender swapping is also certainly something that occurs in *EQ*, one of the more interesting aspects to consider is the way the game may allow access to gender identities that often are socially prohibited or delegitimized offline—a simultaneously sexy and powerful or masculine and beautiful persona. Women in *EverQuest* are constantly engaged in playing with traditional notions of femininity and reformulating gender identities through aspects of the space that are tied directly to its nature as a game. Identity is formulated in relation to formal play elements within the world such that active engagement, embodied agency, and full participation are guiding values for men and women alike. This is a potentially radical framework and one that can challenge stereotypical forms of femininity.

EXPLORATION

The role of this active engagement in the game extends to the way one can interact with its "worldness." One of the notable things MMOG environments (and many computer games in general) offer is the way their construction of worlds lets users actually wander a landscape and explore. Most women I have spoken with express a real enjoyment of engaging with the game as a world and environment. Given the geographic organization of a space like *EverQuest*, users are able to move through an entire world and explore different lands and inhabitants. Gareth R. Schott and Kristy R. Horrell similarly found that girls whose games were engaged with exploration, suggesting that "respondents were focused around the freedom that RPG's gave to exploration of its virtual environment for the accumulation of symbols that possess general life enhancing qualities" (2000, 43). One woman I spoke with recounted her experiences trekking her own Necromancer around the world ("from one end of Norrath to the other") and the peril and excitement such a journey brought. Jackie noted she specifically created a Druid because they "were the ultimate explorers and at that stage of the game I just really wanted to explore." Mary Fuller and Henry Jenkins (1995) have noted the special kind of "landscape" games provide, and MMOGs present some of the clearest examples of movement through elaborate virtual spaces (though with a much richer sense of character and embodiment than early videogames offered).

While men and women alike can enjoy traversing these spaces, women are afforded an experience they are likely not to have had offline. While both the landscape and its creatures might threaten the explorer, in the game space this threat is not based upon gender. Unlike the offline world in which gender often plays a significant role in not only the perception of safety but its actuality, in EQ women may travel knowing they are no more threatened by the creatures of the world than their male counterparts are. While this may seem an odd reassurance, it is far from minor. Risk of travel in-game is tied to more general categories of faction (does a particular town or zone's inhabitants hate your class or race?), power (do the area's creatures know you are more powerful than they or are they confident in their ability to kill you first?), or skill (can you effectively hide, sneak, or pass through undetected?). Because of this gender-neutral approach to threat and safety, there is a kind of freedom of movement that women often do not experience otherwise. It is also the case that as one levels and obtains greater mastery of the game space, zones of free exploration are broadened. An area that was previously quite dangerous to a character was not dangerous because of gender, and eventually it might become accessible with game competency. This is an important pleasure of the game, and many women enjoy extended travel and exploration of the virtual world.

BEYOND PINK GAMES

Typical accounts of women and games tend to focus exclusively on identity, exploration, and socialization. The mid-1990s saw a fair amount of scholarly work, not to mention commercial investment, around the issue of girls and gaming. Justine Cassell and Henry Jenkins's edited collection *From Barbie to Mortal Kombat* (1998), one of the best and most widely cited collections on the subject, offers an excellent snapshot of that period. While some work in the 1990s was notable for its nuanced approach in understanding the relationship between gender and games, much of it presented stereotypical formulations of girls' relationship to technology. In addition, little was done to disentangle the experience of play across age and the life cycle. Research on girls thus often was extrapolated to apply to women. While animated by a deep concern for enfranchising girls into not only computer gaming but technology more generally, such approaches typically suggested that we needed games geared to traditionally feminine interests and sensibilities. This kind of approach is typified, for example, by the perspective that sees women enjoying the socializing or ethical quandaries of games and men the raw power they are able to exert in them (Brunner, Bennett, and Honey 1998). The model is also one in which girls do not particularly enjoy violence or direct competition in games but instead prefer to funnel their energy toward interpersonal issues, indirect competition, environments, puzzles, or character-based genres (Graner Ray 2004; Kafai 1996; Koster 2005; Subrahmanyam and Greenfield 1998).

To this end there were a number of products launched that sought to bring games to a market traditionally underserved by game companies. While titles like Mattel's *Barbie Fashion Designer* stand at one extreme, Girl Games's *Let's Talk about Me* focused on topical life issues. The work of Brenda Laurel and her company Purple Moon probably best exemplifies the developments to come out of this movement. Known for its *Rockett* series of games, Laurel's company sought to design games around interactive narratives as a way of, very basically, engaging girls with computers. Rather than trying to make a gender-inclusive game, the Purple Moon approach was to design for girls "because we wanted to protect the experience as being something girls could own, something that could be theirs, so that they could say, This is mine, this is for me, I own this and you don't get to make fun of it'" (Cassell and Jenkins 1998, 119). The company's *Rockett games* focused on relationships, secrets, identity negotiation, and interpersonal skills. As Laurel writes in *Utopian Entrepreneur:*

I took a lot of heat from some people who call themselves feminists for portraying girl characters who cared about such things as appearance, popularity, belonging, betrayal, and all the other sturm and drang of preadolescent friendship. Some people thought I shouldn't do that because girls shouldn't behave in this way. But they do, you see. And who they become depends a great deal on how they manage their transit through the narrows of girlhood. (Laurel 2001,3)

Not simply meant for fun or entertainment, the intents of products like those from Purple Moon were laden with social and political ambitions.

The approach of the pink-games movement has close ties to work on gender that suggests that women are more inclined to focus on, and prefer to invest in, activities such as caregiving, interpersonal orientations, cooperation, and internal discovery (Chodorow 1978; Gilligan 1982). Of course, all of these are highly valuable activities, but do they accurately reflect a total vision of femininity? As critical work on the subject points out, femininity and the very notion of "woman" is not an identity category that exists separate from considerations of age, race, class, ethnicity, nationality, sexual orientation, or indeed the matrix of practices that constitute the performance of gender (Butler 1990; Collins 2000; Dugger 1991; Halberstam 1998; hooks 1981; Kerber et al. 1986; Lorber 1991; Romero 1992). Does the 12-year-old, middle-class girl negotiate and perform her gender within the same vertices that the 48-year-old, working-class woman does? Are the stakes the same? Or, maybe better put, does the negotiation of those stakes look the same? Does the same girl enact her gender in the same way across her lifespan? Do the practices, the social maps, the various contexts to understanding particular permutations of gender, transfer across all women? While I certainly do not want to suggest we cannot identify some common stereotypes that circulate in the dominant culture about what women and men do, how much those ideas correspond to actual lived practice and experience is another matter. Far too often I have heard students, for example, talk about how women dislike first-person shooters, only to have them quickly follow up by noting that they themselves do enjoy FPS's but "those other women" do not. I have also encountered men who want to suggest that women dislike competition, but those men are stumped when asked to explain that assumption given the women in their lives who play sports or tabletop games. The current models through which we understand women's engagement with games, including one in which women are seen as "intruders" rather than inhabitants of gamer culture, are linked to a much older rhetoric touching on not only issues of women and technology, but their engagement with sports (Bolin and Granskog 2003; Hargreaves 1994; Kay 2003; Scraton and Flintoff 2002; Wajcman 1991). By keeping in mind the historical context, we can begin to draw on past battles (and victories) over the role of women in technology and science, "masculine activities," and claims for active subject positions.

By focusing on the historical pattern of these arguments, and the variability of gender as it intersects with other factors, we can begin to unpack the apparent invisibility of women gamers. For far too long researchers have overlooked the broader structural and social influences on how the category of "gamer" (something women do not always feel authorized to occupy) has been shaped. The overreliance on fairly narrow psychological understandings of femininity has tended to foster diminished examination of the role of marketing, social networks, technical proficiency, and the actual configuration of game devices as artifacts. Echoes of old and familiar "men are hunters, women are gatherers" and "different brains" stories are also on the rise, and we are seeing tenuous sociobiological theories emerge as powerful rhetoric to explain what games women play, or why they do not.[6] Fortunately for both the field and for women gamers, there is an emerging wave of research tackling these more structural and contextual relationships between gender, technology, culture, and games. Work by researchers including Jo Bryce and Jason Rutter (2003), Diane Carr (2005), Aphra Kerr (2003), Gareth Schott and Kirsty Horrell (2000), Helen Kennedy (2002), and Simeon Yates and Karen Littleton (1999) examine everything from the physical design of game consoles like Microsoft's *XBox* to how the circulation of games within social networks highlights paths of entry (and legitimation) into gamer culture.

There is another layer of critique with the pink-game approach, though. It is the notion that good game design originates by asking people what they want. While companies certainly want to avoid alienating a potential audience (something I discuss a bit more regarding avatars), discovering what appeals to a person when it directly intersects with issues like gender is profoundly tricky. The investments in retaining a cohesive performance of one's gender, at least publicly, makes it quite difficult methodologically to tap into the nuances of desire and potential pleasures. Suzanne de Castell and Mary Btyson argue that we cannot untangle the production of "girl games" from the production of gender itself:

The question we urge is simply: Whose interests will be served in making use of these purportedly "essential" differences as a basis for creating "girl-friendly" computer-mediated environments? Most importantly, are we producing tools for girls, or are we producing girls themselves by, as Althusser (1984) would put it, "interpellating" the desire to become the girl? By playing with girlish toys, does the girl learn to become the kind of woman she was always already destined to become? (1998,251-252)

People may not know what they *could* enjoy. Trying to design from gauging existing tastes or play preferences is one of the most conservative approaches and rarely results in innovation. As Jesper Juul has suggested, if ten years ago designers had asked people if they might like to spend time in a game washing dishes or cooking, replies probably would have focused on how boring or uninteresting that would be. And yet *The Sims*, a game that often centers on mundane activities, has proven one of the best-selling titles ever. Juul astutely points out, "What this tells us is that game development and innovation is often about finding that something previously considered dull can actually be interesting, and that in a sense, innovative games are a discussion about what games are" (Juul 2003). The dangers of a design approach that relies on only asking people what they want (which is actually more like a marketing strategy) is even more dramatic when it comes to gender as it often puts all players (men and women, boys and girls) in the position of trying to imagine the pleasures of activities that may very well be prohibited, indeed sanctioned, in their nongaming lives.

NOTES

1. It does not help that within game culture some notion of what "real games" are seems to predominate, often seeing only huge commercial games or first person shooters as "hardcore" enough to warrant being called a "real" game.

2. Available at http://games.yahoo.com.

3. They no longer collect this information upon registration so the figures are based on past data (Daniel James, personal communication via e-mail, 13 February 2005). An interesting comparison remains with the numbers of women in the non-online gaming and console market. Kathryn Wright (2001a) cites a 1998 survey putting women at 43% of computer gamers and 35% of console users. Women often are "lost" in typical surveys on play because the query is formulated in such a way that ownership is the major marker for denoting the player. But it is often the case that women play on

consoles owned by someone else in the household, so changing questions to measure for "secondary users" can produce different results.

4. For some important critiques on the notion of fluid identities and the utopic possibilities often purported, see Lori Kendall (2002), Beth Kolko (2000), and Lisa Nakamura (1995, 2002).

5. Game guides (volunteer player assistants) can only act in their formal helper capacity on a server other than the one they play on.

6. See Bates (2004) for a fairly classic example of the kind of historical-physical-psychological difference story that circulates as an explanatory model. I have also posed some critiques of this (Taylor 2004a).

REFERENCES

Bolin, Anne, and Jane Granskog, eds. 2003. *Athletic intruders: Ethnographic research on women, culture, and exercise.* Albany, NY: State University of New York.

Brunner, Cornelia, Dorthy Bennett, and Margaret Honey. 1998. Girl games and technological desire. In *From Barbie to Mortal Kombat: Gender and computer games,* ed. Justine Cassell and Henry Jenkins, 72–87. Cambridge, MA: The MIT Press.

Butler, Judith. 1990. *Gender trouble: Feminism and the subversion of identity.* New York: Routledge.

Cassell, Justine, and Henry Jenkins, eds. 1998. *From Barbie to Mortal Kombat: Gender and computer games.* Cambridge, MA: The MIT Press.

Chodorow, Nancy. 1978. *The reproduction of mothering: Psychoanalysis and the sociology of gender.* Berkeley: University of California.

Collins, Patricia Hill. 2000. *Black feminist thought: Knowledge, consciousness, and the politics of empowerment.* New York: Routledge.

Dugger, Karen. 1991. Social location and gender-role attitudes: A comparison of black and white women. In *The social construction of gender,* ed. Judith Lorber and Susan A. Farrell. Newbury Park: Sage.

Fuller, Mary, and Henry Jenkins. 1995. Nintendo and new world travel writing: A dialogue. In *Cybersociety: Computer-mediated communication and community,* ed. Steven G. Jones. Thousand Oaks: Sage.

Gilligan, Carol. 1982. *In a different voice: Psychological theory and women's development*. Cambridge, MA: Harvard University Press.

Guernsey, Lisa. 2001. Women play games online in larger numbers than men. *The New York Times*, 4 January. http://www.nytimes.com.

Halberstam, Judith. 1998. *Female masculinity*. Durham: Duke University Press.

Hargreaves, Jennifer. 1994. *Sporting females: Critical issues in the history and sociology of women's sports*. London: Routledge.

hooks, bell. 1981. *Ain't I a woman? Black women and feminism*. Boston: South End Press.

Juul, Jesper. 2003. Just what is it that makes computer games so different, so appealing? The Ivory Tower (April). http://www.igda.org/columns/ivorytower/ivory_Apr03.php.

Kay, Tess. 2003. Sport and gender. In *Sport and society*, ed. Barrie Houlihan. London: Sage.

Kerber, Linda K., Catherine G. Greeno, Eleanor E. Maccoby, Zella Luria, Carol B. Stack, and Carol Gilligan. 1986. On *In a different voice:* An interdisciplinary forum. *Signs: Journal of Women in Culture and Society* 11 (21): 304–333.

Laber, Emily. 2001. Men are from *Quake*, women are from *Ultima. The New York Times*, 11 January. http://www.nytimes.com/.

Laurel, Brenda. 2001. *Utopian entrepreneur*. Cambridge, MA: The MIT Press.

Lorber, Judith. 1991. Dismantling Noah's ark. In *The social construction of gender*, ed. Judith Lorber and Susan A. Farrell. Newbury Park: Sage.

Schott, Gareth R., and Kirsty R. Horrell. 2000. Girl gamers and their relationship with the gaming culture. *Convergence* 6 (4): 36–53.

Scraton, Sheila, and Anne Flintoff. 2002. *Gender and sport: A reader*. New York: Routledge.

Taylor, T. L. 2002. Living digitally: Embodiment in virtual worlds. In *The Social Life of Avatars: Presence and Interaction in Shared Virtual Environments*, ed. Ralph Schroeder. Springer-Verlag, London.

Turkle, Sherry. 1995. *Life on the screen: Identity in the age of the Internet*. New York: Simon & Schuster.

Invent

Taylor begins her chapter by asking you to think about "gamers." What are they like? Who do you imagine or picture? What might they look like? Before reading this chapter, write down your responses to her questions. Then, after you've read, re-read your responses. Would you change any of your responses after reading "Where the Women Are"? Why or why not?

Explore

Choose an advertisement for a popular video or computer game and analyze how it represents gender. Does it seem to target a particular gendered audience? What characteristics—language, images, and so on—of the advertisement seem to indicate that it is targeted to a certain gender? Does the game seem to play into stereotypes about the "typical gamer" or not? Why?

Collaborate

With a group of classmates, choose a game space to inhabit for several weeks. You might choose *World of Warcraft, Second Life, Guild Wars,* and so on. Play as a character of a different gender than you identify with in real life. After your group has played for a while in the game space, talk with each other about the experience of inhabiting a character of a different gender. What was it like? Did others react to you differently? Did you notice that characters of the opposite gender than yours played differently than you did? If you noticed differences, why do you think those differences exist?

MAJOR ASSIGNMENTS

BACKGROUND

Many of the readings in this textbook reflect on the idea of "growing up digital"; that is, these essays describe individuals who have grown up surrounded by technology and have perhaps taken them for granted because of their ubiquity. But each one of us has a story to tell about the impact of technologies on our lives.

ASSIGNMENT

In thinking about the impact of technologies in your life from your childhood on, write an autobiography that details your experiences with technologies and makes a claim about what your interactions with technology say about you as a person today. Identify a specific audience that you will write to: your classmates, your instructor, a friend or parent, or other audience as applicable and structure your autobiography in ways that will appeal to that audience. Throughout your autobiography, use thoughtful plotting, vivid description, and character development to tell a compelling narrative about at least one (perhaps more) significant technological moment, memory, or theme drawn from your life. Base your autobiography on experiences that left a lasting impression on you and that you can use to speak to your audience. Make it clear why your interactions with technology were significant in your life and how they have had an impact on the person that you are today.

QUESTIONS FOR INVENTION

The questions below are meant to offer ideas for responding; you may choose to respond to some or all of these questions. You may not respond to them in order, instead selecting to respond to those questions that are particularly applicable to your story and your audience and choosing an organizational pattern for your autobiography that makes it clear and focused.

- What are some of your earliest memories about technology? Did you use computers, cell phones, music devices, or other technologies as you were growing up? Did you have positive or negative experiences with technology as a young child? Have your parents related any funny or interesting stories about you and technology?

- Have you gravitated toward specific technologies as you have grown older? Are there technologies you no longer use or no longer care for? Among your friends, are you particularly technologically savvy or are you a late adopter of technologies?

- What technologies have you had to learn to use as you've grown older? What technologies are you particularly good at using? What technologies are you still unfamiliar with but would like to learn?

- How do the technologies you use or carry on you reflect your personality, interests, ideas, and values? Have you adapted your technologies to reflect who you are—for example, adding a charm or special ringtone to your cell phone or engraving your iPod?

ABOUT AUTOBIOGRAPHIES

An autobiography is a kind of essay where the author writes about him or herself to communicate to the audience a story that reflects an important aspect of the author's life. As you brainstorm and begin drafting your essay, keep in mind that your autobiography should:

- Focus on a set of clearly defined and well-connected moments, rather than your entire technological life, to convey a specific message and/or emotion to the audience.

- Explore your memories of the experiences, using personal narrative and detailed descriptions, in order to explain the significance of technology in your life to the audience.

- Include concrete details that appeal to the audience's senses.

- Reflect on your experiences to help the audience understand how technology affected you and why these experiences should matter to them.

- You may wish to include visuals such as photographs, clip art, drawings, or similar graphics in your autobiography to help illustrate the technologies that you have discussed.

MAJOR ASSIGNMENT #2:
ANALYZING A SOCIAL NETWORKING PROFILE

BACKGROUND

Online social networking sites like MySpace and Facebook privilege the construction of an individual user profile that is meant to tell viewers something about the individual being profiled.

These profiles therefore paint to friends a picture of an individual through pictures, songs, quotes, factual information, status updates, blogs, and links.

ASSIGNMENT

Choose a public MySpace or Facebook user profile to analyze. You can analyze your own profile, create a new profile for the purposes of this assignment, or choose someone famous (a film star, musician, politician, or similar) who has a public profile. Throughout your analysis, focus on rhetorically analyzing the profile to discover how it reflects aspects of the individual it profiles. You want to argue for a particular way of viewing the profile based on the choices that you have made (or that you believe the author has made, if the profile is not of you). As you compose your essay, consider your argument: What is it that you want to argue about the construction of identity and (e)dentity based on your analysis of this profile? Based on this argument, include a controlling thesis that helps drive the organization of your essay.

QUESTIONS FOR INVENTION IF ANALYZING YOUR OWN PROFILE

The questions below are meant to offer ideas for responding; you may choose to respond to some or all of these questions. You may not respond to them in order, instead selecting to respond to those questions that are particularly applicable to your response and choosing an organizational pattern for your analysis that makes it clear and focused.

How did you choose to fill out the various sections of your profile? What information did you consider most important to communicate to your audience? What information, if any, did you not provide your audience and why? If you change the information in your profile regularly, how do you change it and why?

Who do you envision as your intended audience for your profile? Who do you think reads it? What kind of impression do you believe this audience would get about you based on the information that you have provided? Is there any information that you think might not make sense to a viewer or might be misinterpreted? Why?

If you have included photographs, listed favorites (movies, music, television, books, or activities), or joined groups, how do these profile features add to the construction of your identity in your profile? In other words, how does your default photo reflect what you see as your online identity? How might others view you based on what your favorites, your photos, your groups, or comments on your Wall say about you?

If you have included status updates or blogs, how does the writing in the status updates or blogs help add an additional layer to your (e)dentity? Is your intended audience for your status updates or blogs the same as your intended audience for your overall profile? Why or why not? What specific rhetorical choices (style, tone, language and word choices) have you made as you composed your status updates and blogs?

Finally, consider your privacy settings. What privacy settings have you chosen to use and why? Have you limited access to your profile to certain groups of people? Who have you limited and why? Have privacy settings impacted your ability to show a particular "face" to your audience?

QUESTIONS FOR INVENTION IF ANALYZING ANOTHER'S PROFILE

The questions below are meant to offer ideas for responding; you may choose to respond to some or all of these questions. You may not respond to them in order, instead selecting to respond to those questions that are particularly applicable to your response and choosing an organizational pattern for your analysis that makes it clear and focused.

Who do you think is the intended audience for this profile? What various groups of people do you believe the author intended to view this information? Who do you think actually reads it? Do you believe there are differences between the intended audience and the actual viewers? Why?

Is there any information included in this profile that you think might not make sense to a viewer or might be misinterpreted? Why? Is there anything that does not make sense to you as a viewer or that you do not have enough information to understand?

If the author of this profile has included photographs, listed favorites (movies, music, television, books, or activities), or joined groups, how do these profile features add to the construction of their identity in your profile? In other words, how do the photos, favorites, and groups construct a particular online identity for this individual? How would you characterize this individual's (e)dentity based on what you see in his or her profile?

If the author of this profile has included status updates or blogs, how does the writing in the status updates or blogs help add an additional layer to the individual's (e)dentity? Do you believe you are part of the intended audience for their status updates or blogs? Why or why not? What textual cues help you understand the individual's intended audience?

MAJOR ASSIGNMENT #3: "YOU'RE FIRED!" LEGAL AND ETHICAL RAMIFICATIONS OF LIFE ONLINE

BACKGROUND

Do employers have the right to demand that their employees portray themselves in certain ways online or surveil employees' profile pages? Perhaps not, but this does happen and people have been fired because of their online personas or activities in the past. As Cory Doctorow's story "Scroogled" points out, we never know who may be watching what we are doing online—and we may not know what the ramifications of our actions might be either.

ASSIGNMENT

Imagine that you are an employer and have recently had to talk with an employee about their Facebook profile or your online activities. You ended the communication with the dreaded words, "You're fired." Write a researched argument detailing your stance on the issue of employees being fired for their actions and words online. You may choose to write your researched argument to an audience that would be interested in knowing why you made the choices you did, such as your boss or another higher-up, or possibly to other employees in your company. In your response, draw on the examples of real-life employees who have been fired for their online activities such as Natalie Munroe of Central Bucks East High School, Elaine Liner of *The Phantom Professor* blog, Heather Armstrong of Dooce.com, or Deborah Frisch, formerly of the University of Arizona (or choose local examples from your own community). Be sure to focus on whether or not you believe online social networking profiles should be cause for firings and why. Discuss your opinions on whether it is appropriate for employers to keep track of their employees' actions outside of the workplace and justify your opinion by drawing on legal cases that have been settled in court.

QUESTIONS FOR INVENTION

Your instructor will give you more details about the kind of research you should do as you prepare to write your essay, and he or she may ask you to compile an annotated bibliography of sources as an invention exercise.

- Compile research that examines whether employees have been fired in the past for their writing or actions online, particularly in social networking sites like MySpace or Facebook. Were they able to fight their termination legally? Were they able to keep their jobs?

- You may want to research the legal rights of employees in your state or at your place of employment. Have employees successfully challenged their termination in your state? Are there guidelines for unjust termination?

- Try to find common ground with your audience and make them care about your topic. How can you get your readers to feel empathetic toward your stance and listen to what you have to say? Can you explain to your audience about any special considerations or reasons why you fired your employee? Or describe what other employees can do, such as adhering to a workplace code of conduct, that would ensure similar situations would not happen as often in the future.

MAJOR ASSIGNMENT #4:
EXPLORING AN ONLINE COMMUNITY

BACKGROUND

Many of the readings in this textbook focus on the ways people interact in online communities.

Several readings discuss social networking sites (Donath and boyd; Rott) while others look at online gaming spaces (Taylor). Even Howard Rheingold's article about the Amish focuses on their acceptance of technology. At the heart of each reading is the concept of *community*. This assignment asks you to explore online communities—what they are, what it is like to join one, what it is like to be a member (both from your perspective and from another member's perspective)—and drawing conclusions in a recommendation report about how a member should participate in this community.

ASSIGNMENT

First, you will need to find an online community to join. (This may be a community that is new to you or it may be one that you are already a part of.) At first, you should "lurk" where you watch the interactions of individuals in your community but you do not participate yet yourself. Give yourself enough time to immerse yourself in the community and get a full picture of community interactions: at least several weeks, although over a month is ideal. You may also spend some time looking over archived posts and other materials that reveal the history of this community. Note particularly who seems to be part of your community. Do the same people log in over and over? Are there new people each time? Is there a core group of old-timers and some newer people? Do people of a particular type participate more or less. (For example, do certain genders post more or less often? Certain age groups?)

Similarly, focus on the communication that takes place in this site. Is there lingo or jargon to be learned to communicate effectively? Is there is a FAQ (Frequently Asked Questions) to help new users? How would you characterize the nature of discussions and interactions in this space? Are they full of in jokes? Welcoming to new people? Typically on or off topic?

Next, continue watching what happens in your community, but begin participating (posting discussion topics or questions, chatting, playing, responding to others). Be sure to introduce yourself to your community and let them know who you are and why you have joined. It is important to let the members of the community know that you are interested in writing about the community; ideally, you will introduce yourself as a student who has been watching the community for a while in order to write a recommendation report about the site and interactions within it. Be as transparent as possible; in other words, let the community members know why you've joined—but hopefully you have joined a group that you have an interest in beyond your research, so be sure to point out both your research interests and your personal interests to the group.

If your instructor approves, you can add an additional layer to your recommendation report by interviewing a member of the community about their experiences. Ideally, you will only conduct an interview in a community that you have been participating in for some time so that the members are already familiar with you and your presence; also, the community should be one in which you have felt welcomed. You probably would not want to interview someone who has been hostile toward you! Ask a member of the community, preferably someone who has been a member for a while, if you can interview them about what it is like to be part of the community. Be sure to ask your instructor for approval before seeking to interview a community member; remember that many communities are tight-knit and members might find a researcher's presence in the community to be intrusive. If you receive approval from your instructor to conduct an interview in this community, keep ethical considerations in mind. Always ask your interviewees for consent before interviewing and make sure all interviewees know that you are conducting this research for a class. Offer interviewees the chance to review your work before you turn it in so that they can agree to what you have written about them. If you have any doubts about the success of an interview in your chosen community or if your instructor has requested not to have students conduct interviews, then continue to observe and take notes as you participate in the group, but do not approach specific members of the community for an interview. Your instructor may have you read an article about ethics and interviewing before you begin, such as Katherine Borland's book chapter "'That's Not What I Said': Interpretative Conflict in Oral Narrative Research" or a selection from Ann Blakeslee and Cathy Fleischer's textbook *Becoming a Writing Researcher*.

Finally, write up your experience, drawing on your notes that you have taken during the last few weeks, the interview you've conducted, if applicable, what you've learned from your participation in the community, etc. This write-up should take the form of a recommendation report that describes the best way (in your opinion) to integrate and interact in your particular online community, based on what you have observed and experienced.

RECOMMENDATION REPORTS

Recommendation reports generally draw on research to present an opinion on a topic and recommend a plan of action. Your recommendation report should showcase the research that you have conducted in your online community and clearly recommend "best practices" for participating in that community. In general, your report should include:

- A clear introduction to your online community: What it is; where it can be accessed; and other background information about the community.

- A detailed summary of the primary research that you conducted while observing your community.

- A discussion of your results—what you observed as you participated in your online community and what you believe your results mean (why they are significant).

- Incorporation of your interview transcript, if applicable, in the form of carefully chosen direct quotes, paraphrases, and summaries.

- Finally, a clear set of recommendations for an individual who would like to participate in this online community. Based on your research, what are some of the best practices for interacting in this community? What should new participants be aware of? What, if anything, should participants avoid and why, based on your observations?

MAJOR ASSIGNMENT #5:
REFLECTING ON DEFINITIONS OF DIGITAL NATIVES

BACKGROUND

Authors like John Palfrey, Urs Gasser, and Steven Johnson drew on the term, "digital natives" to talk about today's students' attitudes toward technology. Having grown up surrounded by technology, many academics believe that digital natives effortlessly create mashups and remixes in their sleep after relentlessly creating videos about every aspect of their day that are then posted to YouTube. What do you think? Based on what you have read in this textbook as well consultation of further resources, are the expectations about students today—digital natives—realistic? Or should these definitions be complicated to represent more accurately the typical life of a twenty-first century student?

ASSIGNMENT

First, watch Michael Wesch's video, co-created with students from his class, titled "A Vision of Students Today." You can find it by going to YouTube and typing in the title, "A Vision of Students Today." Then, after reading the pieces about digital natives in this textbook from Palfrey, Gasser, and Johnson, create your own vision of students today either in the form of an audio essay or a video. Your audio essay or video should make an argument about the realities of students today from your point of view: Tell a story and engage in a conversation with the authors referenced above that explains how you feel about their assertions regarding "digital natives."

QUESTIONS FOR INVENTION

You may wish to think through the following questions as you plan your audio essay or video.

Message: What is my proposed message about digital natives and students today? What do I want the person who is listening to this audio essay or watching this video to understand?

Action Step: Do I want to invoke a call to action in my audience? Do I want the person listening or watching to do or think something differently as a result of my piece?

Significance of Issue to the Public: Why it is important that your audience hear from you? What has the previous conversation about digital natives failed to acknowledge or understand? Are there any facts, statistics, or stories that might be useful to share with your audience?

ABOUT AUDIO ESSAYS OR VIDEOS

Effective audio essays and videos use ambient sounds, background music, audio effects, photographs, and video clips to help build their argument. Use these different elements to create an appropriate soundscape for your audio essay or video; incorporate images that add to the rhetorical effectiveness of your argument. Be sure that you do not just read a script but instead try to convey your message to your audience through your performance and other aspects of sound. Keep your audience interested and engaged through your rhetorical choices (voice modulation and tone, pacing, background sounds and music, imagery and color).

(E)DENTITY

(E)DENTITY FILMOGRAPHY

FEATURE FILMS

VIRTUAL REALITY

"Have you ever had a dream, Neo, that you were so sure was real? What if you were unable to wake from that dream? How would you know the difference between the dream world and the real world?" Morpheus asks Neo, the hero of the action thriller *The Matrix*. Many of these films ask us to think about the world that surrounds us: Can we believe it is real? How do we know?

eXistenZ

Directed by David Cronenberg and starring Jennifer Jason Leigh and Jude Law, *eXistenZ* takes place in a series of virtual reality games; the film distorts reality and continuously confronts the characters with the question "Is this real?"

The Matrix

The Matrix also stars Keanu Reeves as the hero Neo, the one person who can free humanity from the virtual reality world named "The Matrix," where humans have been enslaved by artificial intelligence in the form of sentient machines. In the real world, humans are grown in pods and their bioelectrical energy is harvested by the machines to continue running. *The Matrix* was followed by the sequels *The Matrix Reloaded* and *The Matrix Revolutions*.

The Thirteenth Floor

Hannon Fuller, inventor of a virtual reality system that features Los Angeles in the 1930s, is murdered; before he died, however, he left an important message in his virtual reality world. Suspected of Fuller's murder, Douglas

Hall, played by Craig Bierko, must find the message and defend his innocence. A twist ending makes the viewer question reality.

Tron

Jeff Bridges is computer hacker Kevin Flynn, who attempts to hack into his former employer's computer system, ENCOM, to find evidence that his work was stolen. Instead, he is digitized by the ENCOM Master Control Program (MCP) and transported into the digital world ruled by the MCP. With the help of a security program named Tron, Flynn fights to destroy the MCP. Nearly thirty years later, the sequel, *Tron: Legacy*, was released.

Tron: Legacy

When Kevin Flynn was pulled into the ENCOM computer system, he left behind a son, Sam; now nearly thirty, Sam begins investigating his father's disappearance and unintentionally is drawn into the same game system; he discovers his father has been held captive in the system and must rescue him.

Virtuosity

Russell Crowe and Denzel Washington are pitted against each other in this action adventure film where Crowe, playing SID v 6.7, a virtual reality program created from the profiles of hundreds of sadistic, intelligent and dangerous serial killers, attempts to break into the real world; only Washington, as Lieutenant Parker Barnes, can stop him.

COMPUTER HACKING

Looking for weak spots and security holes, hackers attempt to gain entry into computer systems for a variety of reasons—to take those systems down; to showcase the weaknesses; or sometimes just to prove they can. Many Hollywood films have focused on computer hacking, often portraying it as glamorous and thrilling, but often dangerous as well.

Hackers

Dade Murphy, a hacker known by his alias "Zero Cool," teams up with friends and fellow hackers to battle computer security expert Eugene Belford, played by Fisher Stevens, a former hacker who has been stealing money from the Ellingson Mineral Company and is now trying to pin the crime on Zero Cool and his friends.

Johnny Mnemonic

Based on a short story by cyberpunk author William Gibson, *Johnny Mnemonic* stars Keanu Reeves as the title character, a data courier whose package is stored inside his head. Pursued by Yakuza assassins, he must download the data inside his head before he dies.

The Net

As Angela Bennett, Sandra Bullock plays a reclusive systems analyst whose identity is stolen after she is given a strange computer disk with secret information on it. She must fight to regain her true identity and expose the Praetorians, the cyberterrorists who are trying to stop her.

Sneakers

Robert Redford's character Martin Bishop is a hacker approached by the National Security Agency to recover a black box in exchange for clearing his past crimes. With a team of fellow hackers, Bishop discovers the box but also learns it is far more powerful than they thought after an old friend turned rival, Cosmo (Ben Kingsley), tries to steal the box for himself.

Swordfish

John Travolta, Hugh Jackman, and Halle Berry star in this action film. Jackman is a divorced "superhacker" named Stanley Jobson who just wants his daughter back; Travolta plays the villain, Gabriel Shear, who with the help of Berry's character Ginger seduces Jobson into breaking into a bank to steal several million dollars.

WarGames

Teenager David Lightman (Matthew Broderick) connects to a intelligent supercomputer called WOPR, War Operation Plan Response, that runs nuclear war simulations. While Lightman believes he is playing a computer game called "Global Thermonuclear War," WOPR is actually simulating Soviet attacks on the United States, potentially triggering World War III.

SOCIAL NETWORKING

While not many feature films today focus on social networking, the success of the documentary drama *The Social Network*, which won several awards at the Golden Globes and was nominated for eight Academy Awards, may soon change that.

The Social Network

Based on the book *The Accidental Billionaires* by Ben Mezrich, *The Social Network* is a dramatized version of the real-life beginnings of Facebook; Mark Zuckerberg, played by Jesse Eisenberg, faces dual lawsuits after Facebook begins to grow in popularity.

BLOGGING

Dear Me: A Blogger's Tale

Because of her fear of saying the wrong thing, Samantha (Sarah Thompson) begins a blog called "Dear Me" where she can work out some of her anxieties. However, the blog is discovered by her co-workers, who can now read all about her romantic interest in the head of public relations for the French client of the company she works for. Samantha must figure out how to contain her blog and keep her job.

Julie and Julia

Julie Powell's year-long attempt to cook every recipe in Julia Child's *Mastering the Art of French Cooking* was chronicled in Powell's blog *Julie and Julia*, then made into a motion picture with Amy Adams (playing blogger Powell) and Meryl Streep (as Julia Child).

Redacted

Director Brian De Palma's fictional drama centers on the 2006 Mahmudiyah killings and gang rape of a fourteen-year-old girl in Iraq; the film takes the form of a documentary through its use of clips meant to look like soldiers' personal videos as well as surveillance footage, news clips, webcams, and so on. Controversial and graphic, *Redacted* is an intriguing look at how media reports are filtered and presented to viewers.

DOCUMENTARIES

The following documentaries deal with video and computer gaming, online celebrity, social networking, and blogging.

VIDEO AND COMPUTER GAMING

Life 2.0

This documentary follows a group of residents in Second Life, a virtual world/online game space, and focuses on how these residents' real lives were shaped by their activities and interactions in Second Life. Director Jason Spingarn-Koff created his own Second Life account and avatar and spent over three years fully immersing himself in the world he explores in *Life 2.0*.

Second Skin

Second Skin showcases seven individuals whose lives have been transformed by massively multiplayer online role-playing games (MMORPGs) like EverQuest and World of Warcraft. The documentary discusses several controversial and intriguing aspects of MMORPGs, including gold farming, disability, in-game relationships, and addiction.

The King of Kong: A Fistful of Quarters

The rivalry between champion Donkey Kong players Billy Mitchell and Steve Wiebe is explored in this engaging documentary that features a great deal of suspense, humor, and Donkey Kong action.

ONLINE CELEBRITY

Butterflies

The six stars of *Butterflies* are all prominent YouTube "weblebrities"; after the phenomenal success of singer Justin Bieber, discovered via YouTube, others want a taste of the same success. The distribution of Butterflies is itself an experiment in the power of social media to gain exposure for a film; not only has director Ester Brym made *Butterflies* available for rent via Netflix, the film also takes advantage of YouTube's pay-to-rent option.

Starsuckers

The tagline for this documentary is "an exposé of a culture obsessed by celebrity" and it delivers on its promise to show how our obsession with fame drives tabloids to cut corners on fact-checking. Director Chris Atkins set out to game the tabloid system by creating fictitious tales about well-known figures. Not only were many of the stories about celebrities such as Avril Lavigne, Amy Winehouse, and Russell Brand printed in several London tabloids, other publications reprinted the stories without attempting to verify the information first.

SOCIAL NETWORKING
Catfish

Can we trust that the person we are communicating with online is who they say they are? *Catfish* illustrates how the anonymity of the Internet can impact the relationships we form in social media as we watch Nev, the brother of co-director Ariel Schulman, find out more about his Facebook friends Abby and Megan.

BLOGGING
Blogumentary

Blogumentary is currently available through Google Video and is free for non-profit educational use. It features interviews with several bloggers, including Jeff Jarvis, Rebecca Blood, John Hinderaker, David Weinberger, and others.

WORKS CITED

Carr, Nicholas. "The Love Song of J. Alfred Prufrock's Avatar." *Rough Type*, 15 May 2006. Web. 25 Dec. 2010.

Cooper, Robbie, Tracy Spaight, and Julian Dibbell. *Alter Ego: Avatars and Their Creators*. London: Chris Boot, 2007.

Deresiewicz, William. "Faux Friendship." *The Chronicle Review*. The Chronicle of Higher Education, 6 Dec. 2009. Web. 25 Dec. 2010.

Doctorow, Cory. "Scroogled." *Radaronline.com*. 27 Oct. 2008. Web.

Donath, Judith and boyd, danah. "Public Displays of Connection." *BT Technology Journal* 22.4 (Oct. 2004): 71-82. Print.

Gladwell, Malcolm. "Small Change: Why the Revolution Will Not Be Tweeted." *The New Yorker*, 4 Oct. 2010. Web. 25 Dec. 2010.

Johnson, Steven. "Dawn of the Digital Natives." *The Guardian*, 7 Feb. 2008. Web. 25 Dec. 2010.

Kiesow, Damon. "Twitter was an Imperfect News Channel during Giffords Coverage." *Poynter.org*, 10 Jan. 2011. Web. 14 Jan. 2011.

Kolbert, Elizabeth. "The Things People Say: Rumors in an Age of Unreason." *The New Yorker*, 2 Nov. 2009. Web. 25 Dec. 2010.

Munroe, Randall. "Online Communities." *XKCD*, 2007. Web. 13 Feb. 2011.

---. "Online Communities 2." XKCD, 2010. Web. 13 Feb. 2011.

Palfrey, John and Gasser, Urs. *Born Digital: Understanding the First Generation of Digital Natives*. New York: Basic Books, 2008. 17-31. Print.

Puente, Maria. "What Would Shakespeare Tweet?" *USA Today*, 10 June 2006. 1D. Print.

Rheingold, Howard. "Look Who's Talking." *Wired* 7.1 (Jan. 1999). Web. 25 Dec. 2010.

Rott, Nathan. "Homeless Man in D.C. Uses Facebook, Social Media to Advocate for Others Like Him." *The Washington Post*, 13 Dec. 2010. Web. 25 Dec. 2010.

Sullivan, Andrew. "Why I Blog." *The Atlantic*, Nov. 2008. Web. 25 Dec. 2010.

Taylor, T. L. *Play Between Worlds: Exploring Online Game Culture*. Cambridge, MA: MIT Press, 2006. 93-102. Print.

Turkle, Sherry. "Always-On/Always-On-You: The Tethered Self." *Handbook of Mobile Communication Studies*. Ed. James E. Katz. Cambridge, MA: MIT Press, 2008. 121-137. Print.

Wortham, Jenna. "As Facebook Users Die, Ghosts Reach Out." *The New York Times*, 17 July 2010. Web. 13 Feb. 2011.